OECD Reviews on Local Job Creation

Engaging Employers and Developing Skills at the Local Level in Northern Ireland, United Kingdom

This work is published under the responsibility of the Secretary-General of the OECD. The opinions expressed and arguments employed herein do not necessarily reflect the official views of OECD member countries.

This document, as well as any data and any map included herein, are without prejudice to the status of or sovereignty over any territory, to the delimitation of international frontiers and boundaries and to the name of any territory, city or area.

Please cite this publication as:
OECD (2019), *Engaging Employers and Developing Skills at the Local Level in Northern Ireland, United Kingdom*, OECD Reviews on Local Job Creation, OECD Publishing, Paris.
https://doi.org/10.1787/9789264311626-en

ISBN 978-92-64-31161-9 (print)
ISBN 978-92-64-31162-6 (pdf)

Series: OECD Reviews on Local Job Creation
ISSN 2311-2328 (print)
ISSN 2311-2336 (online)

The statistical data for Israel are supplied by and under the responsibility of the relevant Israeli authorities. The use of such data by the OECD is without prejudice to the status of the Golan Heights, East Jerusalem and Israeli settlements in the West Bank under the terms of international law.

Photo credits: Cover © Pykha/Thinkstock by Getty Image/Fotolia

Corrigenda to OECD publications may be found on line at: *www.oecd.org/about/publishing/corrigenda.htm*.
© OECD 2019

You can copy, download or print OECD content for your own use, and you can include excerpts from OECD publications, databases and multimedia products in your own documents, presentations, blogs, websites and teaching materials, provided that suitable acknowledgement of OECD as source and copyright owner is given. All requests for public or commercial use and translation rights should be submitted to *rights@oecd.org*. Requests for permission to photocopy portions of this material for public or commercial use shall be addressed directly to the Copyright Clearance Center (CCC) at *info@copyright.com* or the Centre français d'exploitation du droit de copie (CFC) at *contact@cfcopies.com*.

Foreword

Local vocational education and training (VET) programmes serve as a valuable skills development pathway to improve the transition from school to work. Within the VET system, apprenticeship programmes mix on-the-job training with classroom-based learning.

Expanding the availability of quality apprenticeship programmes can provide employers with a skilled workforce that is more agile in a rapidly evolving global economy while also supporting new employment opportunities for disadvantaged groups. Efforts to improve the quality of apprenticeships and other work-based training opportunities can contribute to regional economic development objectives by building the competitiveness of local growth sectors.

In collaboration with the Northern Ireland Department for the Economy, the OECD's Local Economic and Employment Development (LEED) Programme has conducted a review on engaging employers and developing skills at the local level in Northern Ireland (United Kingdom). Northern Ireland is looking to transform its labour market through the *Success through Skills* and *Securing Our Success* strategies. Both of these strategies aim to make the education and training system more responsive to the labour market of today and tomorrow.

This OECD report examines how to better engage employers in skills development opportunities within the workplace while shedding light on a number of key policy principles to guide action around business-education partnerships. As part of this study, the OECD conducted a survey of employers in partnership with the Chamber of Commerce and the Department for the Economy, to ascertain their views on the skills development system as well as their perceptions of the strengths and challenges facing apprenticeships. Best practices examples are also highlighted throughout the report to illustrate programme design principles that can guide future action in Northern Ireland.

This report was approved by the Directing Committee of the Co-operative Action Programme on Local Economic and Employment Development (LEED) in November 2018.

Acknowledgements

This report has been prepared by the Centre for Entrepreneurship, SMEs, Regions and Cities (CFE), led by Lamia Kamal-Chaoui, Director. This work was conducted as part of the OECD's Local Economic and Employment Development (LEED) Programme.

The project on engaging employers and developing skills at the local level in Northern Ireland, United Kingdom is coordinated by Jonathan Barr, Head of the Employment and Skills Unit within the Local Employment, Skills and Social Innovation (LESI) Division of CFE under the supervision of Sylvain Giguère, Head of Division. The principal authors are Michela Meghnagi (OECD), Pierre Georgin (OECD), Jonathan Barr (OECD) and Maureen O'Reilly (independent consultant). Beatriz Jambrina-Canseco (OECD) and Alessandro Kandiah (OECD) also contributed to this report through statistical analysis. Janine Treves provided editorial assistance while Pilar Philip coordinated the publication process.

OECD colleagues from other Directorates provided valuable input and feedback on the development of this report. They include Anthony Mann from the Directorate of Education and Skills and Katherine Mullock from the Directorate of Employment, Labour and Social Affairs.

Special thanks should be given to Michael Gould, Director, Skills Strategy Division, within the Department for the Economy who coordinated the project within Northern Ireland. The OECD would like to thank senior officials within the Department for the Economy, the Department of Education, Invest NI, and the Department of Communities who were involved in different stages of the project and provided comments on draft versions of this report. Lastly, the OECD would like to thank the Northern Ireland Chamber of Commerce for its support in implementing a skills survey to employers.

Table of contents

Acronyms and Abbreviations 10
Executive Summary 11
Assessment and Recommendations 15
    Working closer with employers for better local labour market outcomes 15
    Better using skills in the workplace 17
    Leveraging regional intelligence to inform policy development 19
    The state of training and programme implementation 19

Chapter 1. Recent economic and labour market trends in Northern Ireland 23
    Set the context 24
    Key government departments implementing employment and skills policies 36
    Conclusions 41
    References 42

Chapter 2. Understanding firm dynamics and skills in Northern Ireland 45
    The profile of Northern Irish firms 46
    The incidence and typology of vacancies 48
    Training provision 51
    Results from the OECD Survey of Northern Ireland firms 52
    Conclusions 59
    References 59

Chapter 3. Implementing employer engagement strategies in Northern Ireland 61
    Understanding how employers are engaging with government on skills needs 62
    Better gearing the skills system to the labour market 64
    Better anticipating future skills needs of Northern Ireland 70
    Promoting inclusive growth in the labour market 72
    Employer engagement in delivering VET at the local level 74
    Improving work organisation, job design and skills utilisation in the workplace 80
    References 87

Figures

Figure 1.1. GVA annual growth rate, United Kingdom and Northern Ireland, 2006 – 2016 24
Figure 1.2. GVA per capita, UK countries, 2006-2016 25
Figure 1.3. GVA per capita, sub-regions of Northern Ireland, 2006-2016 26
Figure 1.4. GVA per capita annual growth rate, sub-regions of Northern Ireland, 2000-2016 26
Figure 1.5. Gross Value Added per filled job, 2016 27
Figure 1.6. Share of total GVA by industry at current basic prices, United Kingdom and Northern
    Ireland, 2015 28

Figure 1.7. People in employment by country of birth in Northern Ireland, 2008 and 2016 29
Figure 1.8. Employment rate, United Kingdom, Northern Ireland, EU-28 and OECD, 2006 and 2016 30
Figure 1.9. Employment rate, Northern Irish LGDs, 2016 31
Figure 1.10. Unemployment rate, selected European countries, 2007-2017 32
Figure 1.11. Youth unemployment rate, selected European countries, 2007-2017 32
Figure 1.12. Long-term unemployment rate, selected European countries, 2007-2017 33
Figure 1.13. Economic inactivity rate, UK countries, 2007-2017 34
Figure 1.14. Share of the labour force by educational attainment, United Kingdom and Northern Ireland, 2007 and 2017 35
Figure 1.15. Share of the population aged 15-64 by educational attainment, Northern Irish LGDs, 2016 35
Figure 1.16. Use of apprenticeships across OECD countries, 2015 38
Figure 1.17. ApprenticeshipsNI starts by age groups, 2013-2017 39
Figure 1.18. ApprenticeshipsNI starts by gender, 2013-2017 39
Figure 1.19. Main fields of training for men, 2013-2017 40
Figure 1.20. Main fields of training for women, 2013-2017 40
Figure 1.21. Number of participants on ApprenticeshipsNI 2013 and ApprenticeshipsNI 2017 by Local Government District 41
Figure 2.1. Sectoral composition of firms, United Kingdom and Northern Ireland, 2017 46
Figure 2.2. Geographical area in which the establishment's goods/services are primarily sold/serviced to the population, UK countries, 2017 47
Figure 2.3. Share of enterprises by broad funding/profit typology, UK countries, 2017 47
Figure 2.4. Vacancies by type, UK countries, 2017 49
Figure 2.5. Skill shortage vacancies over time, UK countries, 2011-2017 50
Figure 2.6. Incidence of vacancies by occupation, United Kingdom and Northern Ireland, 2017 51
Figure 2.7. Type of training provided, UK countries, 2017 52
Figure 2.8. Firm distribution by employment size, Northern Ireland 53
Figure 2.9. Skills needed to improve the productivity of employees, Northern Ireland 54
Figure 2.10. Reasons for not offering apprenticeships, Northern Ireland 55
Figure 2.11. Expected benefits from offering apprenticeships, Northern Ireland 56
Figure 2.12. Concerns about apprenticeship programmes currently in place, Northern Ireland 57
Figure 3.1. High-performance work practices across OECD countries 82
Figure 3.2. Product market strategies, UK countries, 2015 83
Figure 3.3. Share of enterprises that introduced new methods of organising work responsibilities, NUTS2 regions of the UK, 2012-2014 84

Boxes

Box 1.1. Impact of Brexit on the Northern Irish labour market 29
Box 1.2. ApprenticeshipsNI 37
Box 2.1. The UK Employers Skills Survey 48
Box 2.2. The Employer Perspective Survey 54
Box 2.3. The Apprenticeship Levy 58
Box 3.1. Sector Training Councils in Northern Ireland 62
Box 3.2. STEM champions in Northern Ireland: Gearing to the skills system to emerging and innovative sectors 63
Box 3.3. Careers Advisory Forum in Northern Ireland 65
Box 3.4. The Skills Barometer 71

Box 3.5. Implementing a local employment and skills strategy in Northern Ireland 76
Box 3.6. Area Learning Communities 77
Box 3.7. The Council for Curriculum, Examinations and Assessment 78
Box 3.8. The UK Business Productivity Review 81
Box 3.9. The Curriculum Hub initiative 85

Follow OECD Publications on:

 http://twitter.com/OECD_Pubs

 http://www.facebook.com/OECDPublications

 http://www.linkedin.com/groups/OECD-Publications-4645871

 http://www.youtube.com/oecdilibrary

 http://www.oecd.org/oecddirect/

This book has...

A service that delivers Excel® files from the printed page!

Look for the *StatLinks* at the bottom of the tables or graphs in this book. To download the matching Excel® spreadsheet, just type the link into your Internet browser, starting with the *http://dx.doi.org* prefix, or click on the link from the e-book edition.

Acronyms and Abbreviations

DE	Department of Education
DfE	Department for the Economy
GVA	Gross Value Added
LEED	Local Economic and Employment Development
NEET	Not in Employment, Education or Training
NGO	Non-Governmental Organisation
NI	Northern Ireland, United Kingdom
NUTS	Nomenclature of Territorial Units for Statistics
OECD	Organisation for Economic Co-operation and Development
PIAAC	Programme for the International Assessment of Adult Competencies
PISA	Programme for International Student Assessment
SES	Socio-Economic Status
SME	Small and Medium-sized Enterprise
STEM	Science, Technology, Engineering and Mathematics
VET	Vocational Education and Training
UK	United Kingdom

Executive Summary

The Northern Ireland economy has recovered relatively well after the 2008 economic recession, with the unemployment rate sitting at 4.7% in 2017, close to the pre-crisis level. While unemployment is improving, Northern Ireland still has an economic inactivity rate of 28%, which remains persistently above the average of 22% for the United Kingdom (UK). Globalisation, automation and digitalisation will continue to change labour market demands as well as the skills required of people entering employment. Apprenticeship programmes can reduce skills mismatches, and provide a smoother transition into the labour market.

The skills system has been through a number of significant changes with the merger and expansion of local colleges as well as the merger of government departments in Northern Ireland. The introduction of the National Apprenticeship Levy in the UK has also altered the incentives to invest in skills development opportunities. There have been some positive initiatives to engage employers in a formal manner through the Strategic Advisory Forum. A number of new programmes such as Assured Skills and Higher Level Apprenticeships also aim to build higher-level skills opportunities.

These actions have contributed to attracting both individuals and employers into apprenticeship programmes. With 6 500 apprenticeship training starts registered in 2016-17, participation rates have increased by 25% since 2013-14. The share of those in the labour force with tertiary education was 38.4% in 2017, up significantly from 30.2% in 2007. Yet the share of the labour force with only primary education is higher than the UK average (20.9% in Northern Ireland compared to 16.7% in the UK).

The vast majority of firms in Northern Ireland are SMEs, and among them 88% have fewer than 10 employees. Small and micro firms often have particular challenges in upskilling their employees. Around 30% of employers surveyed for this report cite a lack of training capacity as the main reason for not taking part in an apprenticeship programme. About 80% of employers who offer apprenticeships note that they have maintained their apprentices as full-time employees following training. This demonstrates the value of apprenticeships in increasing employability and leading to a lasting and stable job.

Some Further Education Colleges are taking innovative actions to better align their programmes to employer demand. For example, Belfast Metropolitan College has recently established an employer engagement unit to support more direct outreach. Local governments in Northern Ireland are also increasingly active in reaching out to employers about their skills needs. A number of District Councils have developed Employability and Skills Strategies that promote partnerships within their catchment area and include a strong focus on engaging employers about their skills needs.

The following recommendations can guide future action in Northern Ireland:

Improving the quality and effectiveness of apprenticeships

- **Ensure a flexible training system with a focus on quality:** More modular and part-time training opportunities should be offered to increase participation in apprenticeship programmes in Northern Ireland. This would provide more flexible learning opportunities for individuals to participate in apprenticeships.

- **Increase female participation in the apprenticeship system:** Currently, 38% of apprentices are female. The Department for the Economy should aim to increase the number of females participating in apprenticeships through targeted outreach and marketing programmes.

- **Setting clear targets and goals to improve apprenticeship completions:** About 34% of students dropped out of their apprenticeship programme in 2015-16. There is a lack of data on the social background and the reasons why individuals might drop-out. Counselling, information about career choices and regular discussions with apprentices would support completion.

- **Strengthen career guidance for young people moving from secondary school into the labour market:** Apprenticeships remain a "second choice" pathway for many young people despite the presence of a number of high quality job opportunities. The Department for the Economy, Invest NI, and the Department of Education should enhance collaboration with the goal of creating a robust career guidance system that provides quality information on the jobs available through apprenticeship training.

Enhancing collaboration with employers

- **Northern Ireland can strengthen local networks among employers:** Further efforts can be made to encourage coalitions of employers to network on a regional or sector basis. This can encourage firms to collaboratively identify training needs while also ensuring there is enough demand to offer training at a local vocational education and training organisation.

- **Explore more innovative ways to support SMEs or "harder to reach" employers:** Intermediaries and brokers can help in reducing the administrative barriers to apprenticeship participation. Employer education programmes can also raise awareness about the value of training. The Government could introduce direct marketing campaigns and outreach to build public awareness among SMEs about apprenticeship training.

- **A focus on the better use of skills in the workplace can improve job quality at the local level:** Government in Northern Ireland should continue to build evidence about the benefits of skills use policies while also identifying and sharing existing best practices among firms in Northern Ireland. Government should look to encourage more management and leadership training among firms.

Strengthening the role of local government

- **Examine the role of local councils in better gearing training to demand:** Government should consider the establishment of a Local Council Employer Engagement Group, which could be tasked with identifying how to improve the overall local coordination of public services, while identifying best practices among Local Councils in engaging employers.

- **Northern Ireland should aim to foster local skills ecosystems:** The Government could look to encourage the development of local skills ecosystems, which is a cluster of firms working horizontally across a value chain, with the education and training system to foster knowledge exchange and coordination. Skills ecosystems are more likely to occur within a region or sector where firms come together through intermediaries to pursue initiatives such as technical training, which is of mutual interest and benefit.

- **Develop robust local labour market information:** Government should produce more relevant and timely local labour market information on jobs, skills, and economic development trends. This information can be used inform individuals, firms, and governments on future skills development opportunities in Northern Ireland.

Assessment and Recommendations

Northern Ireland has made significant strides to improve the overall engagement of employers with the skills system. The *Success through Skills and Securing Our Success* strategies implemented new initiatives to 'put employers in the driving seat'. Achieving such ambitious objectives requires a responsive education and training system that prepares the workforce for the skills needed in today and tomorrow's labour market. Automation and digitalisation will continue to alter the labour market in Northern Ireland, requiring new and innovative approaches to training targeted to both youth entering the labour market as well as existing workers in at risk jobs.

Working closer with employers for better local labour market outcomes

Apprenticeship starts in Northern Ireland have improved steadily but there is greater room for female participation

While vocational education and training participation rates are low compared to other regions of the OECD, there has been a recent participation increase in apprenticeship programmes. Apprenticeships NI aims to provide eligible individuals with the opportunity to take part in a Level 2 or Level 3 qualification where the apprentice is within paid employment from day one. The total number of apprentices has been steadily increasing since 2013 from 5 203 apprenticeship starts in to 6 499 in 2016-17.

Males account for a significant share of participation in apprenticeship programmes in Northern Ireland, representing 62% of current participants. While there has been an increase in the share of women participating in apprenticeship programmes, there is a clear opportunity to bring more gender balance to these participation numbers.

Northern Ireland can strengthen local networks among employers...

Northern Ireland has made a number of significant commitments to encourage employers to become more involved in steering skills training and delivery at the local level. Furthermore, the government has made a commitment to increase the number of work-based training opportunities that are available to give workers more access to skills upgrading programmes. Progress has been made through a number of government initiatives and forums with the goal of better aligning government interventions/programmes to demand. There have been some positive initiatives to engage employers in a formal manner through the Strategic Advisory Forum and the Sectoral Partnerships. Invest NI also play a significant role in strengthening collaboration among employers both within and outside the UK. A number of new programmes such as Assured Skills and Higher Level Apprenticeships also aim to build higher-level skills opportunities.

Going forward, further efforts can be made to build networks or coalitions of employers within a local area or a region or based on sector demand. Networking among employers is critical to develop a common understanding of the shared skills challenges while also providing clearer directions to government on how policies and programmes can deliver better results. Sector approaches to employer engagement are important in fostering cooperation between training providers and employers while also ensuring occupational and qualification standards align with industry. Northern Ireland may wish to re-visit the *Success through Skills* employer engagement plan that was previously introduced in 2012. The chambers of commerce, sector skills councils, as well as sector training councils have an important role to play in coordinating and advocating for a broad range of interests among employers.

...and explore more innovative ways to support SMEs or "harder to reach" employers

SMEs are a critical driver of job creation within Northern Ireland, representing about 75% of total employment and 80% of Northern Ireland's gross value added. SMEs represent a key pillar within a thriving local economy and regularly engage vocational education and training providers, and employment services. However, SMEs and even more micro enterprises often face unique and specific barriers to engaging in training opportunities given their smaller size.

Fears of poaching often limit their participation in workplace training opportunities. In many cases, SMEs also lack a human resources function that can undertake strategic human resources planning and engage in the administrative requirements of an apprenticeship programme. Northern Ireland should examine its suite of policy and programmes to SMEs as regards skills training, especially apprenticeships with the goal of providing customised support to these firms, which are often the hardest to reach.

Other OECD countries may offer interesting lessons for Northern Ireland going forward. In Australia and Norway, group training organisations are used as an intermediary bodies to manage the apprenticeship contract directly with the government. This shifts the legal obligation and administrative burden to these collective organisations, who are able to use economies of scale to offer a full suite of training services and supports to SMEs. It also enables flexible apprenticeship frameworks, where an individual apprentice can work across firms within a sector or place gaining several different workplace experiences. It can also increase the incentives for employers to participate in training because they do not have to employ the apprentice on a permanent basis.

Employer education programmes can raise awareness of the value of training

Targeting the hardest to reach employers also involves direct marketing campaigns and outreach to build public awareness about the value of investing in a skilled workforce. Many employers will operate their local business without understanding the full benefits of participating in apprenticeships and other work-based training opportunities, which enhance the productive capacity of a company while also improving the retention of employees.

In many cases, it can be helpful to have employers mentor other firms about the benefits of training. Advertising through social media, job boards or specialist websites are some of the activities that can be used to get information to employers. Sector Skills Councils and Sector Training Councils can play a role in this area but this requires that they expand their coverage and scope to other employers who do not actively participate in the Northern Ireland skills system.

Northern Ireland could look to lessons from other regions of the UK, which have established local apprenticeship hubs, which play a key role in marketing apprenticeship programmes to employers, while also serving as a key coordination interface between public services and employers. In Manchester and Leeds, local apprenticeship hubs have been successful in increasing participation in apprenticeship programmes while also offering coordinated support to SMEs. Lessons from the Leeds City apprenticeship hub highlight that local SMEs often found a fragmented advice and guidance system, which limits their knowledge about where to go to participate in apprenticeship programmes as well as the administrative requirements of participation.

Better using skills in the workplace

Enhance management and leadership training

Success through Skills highlights the importance of up-skilling the existing workforce and to look at how companies are managing human capital. Better managed companies have employees who are often more productive in their job. Previously, the Department for the Economy has introduced a number of initiatives targeted to management and leadership training, including the Management Analysis and Planning Programme, the Management Leadership Development Programme as well as the INTRO programme. Together with Invest NI, the Department for the Economy also previously developed an integrated framework for management and leadership within companies. These are welcome developments, which can further develop important and growing sectors within Northern Ireland.

Organisations need to foster participative employee relations in order to build trust so that employees will learn. Furthermore, company reward systems need to support learning and support team-based work organisation. Other OECD countries may have useful models that could be adapted in Northern Ireland. For example, in Belgium, practices labs for workforce innovation were set-up in the Province of Limburg to foster networking among managers to affect change and discuss new ways of better engaging employees within the firm on production and management practices.

A focus on skills utilisation approaches can improve the quality of jobs locally

Most skills policies have been focused on the supply side – that is – they assume that producing a workforce with a higher number of qualifications will improve economic outcomes. The challenges with this approach is that it assumes that the jobs available in a local economy are of sufficient quality and fit the qualifications being produced by the education system. It is increasingly important to look at the quality of employment within the labour market and how public policies can be designed to shape the demand for skills and move companies into higher value added economic activities.

Skills utilisation concerns the extent to which skills are effectively applied in the workplace to maximise employer and individual performance. As such it involves a mix of policies including work organisation, job design, technology adaptation, innovation, employee-employer relations, human resource development practices and business product market strategies. It is often at the local level where the interface of these factors can best be addressed. Policies which aim to improve skills use in the workplace can help address the multi-faceted challenges many local economies are facing and contribute to national productivity and inclusive growth objectives.

Skills use is generally associated with High-Performance Work Practices, which include such things as employee award programmes, flexible job descriptions, regular performance appraisals as well as mentoring and leadership development courses in the workplace. About 20% of jobs in Northern Ireland are characterised by high levels of High-Performance Work Practices, well below that of OECD countries like Sweden, Austria, Finland and Denmark.

Northern Ireland could consider a number of policy options going forward. The government could consider the establishment of a dedicated agency in Northern Ireland, which would aim to build awareness, evidence, and identify existing best practices. This agency could be modelled on the former United Kingdom Commission for Employment and Skills that brought together a leading group of employers to advocate and identify policy solutions on skills utilisation. Another option would be to examine specific financing supports (e.g. tax credits or grants) that could be provided to employers to participate in workforce innovation programmes. Lastly, lesson from other OECD countries demonstrate the importance of leveraging employer networks, who can incentivise this type of behaviour through their local supply chain management practices. For example, large employers in Korea often work in consortiums with SMEs to provide leadership education with the goal of improving workplace relations with firms.

Employee resource groups might also be a model in which Northern Ireland could draw inspiration for future programme development. Employee resource groups are networks of employees that aim to foster diversity and inclusion in the workplace while also providing valuable advice to companies on issues related to human resources and organisational management. In the United States, many private sector companies have created such groups to foster great employer-employee dialogue while providing workers more opportunities to problem solve, thinking innovatively, and develop leadership skills.

Northern Ireland should aim to foster local skills ecosystems

Recently, the Department for the Economy has published its *Draft Industrial Strategy for Northern Ireland – Economy 2030* with the goal of creating 80 000 new jobs by 2030. This strategy also identifies a number of critical sectors for growth including digital and creative technologies, life and health sciences, financial and professional services, as well as advanced manufacturing and engineering.

To improve the quality of jobs at the local level, Northern Ireland could look to encourage the development of local skills ecosystem, which is a cluster of firms working horizontally across a value chain with the education and training system to foster knowledge exchange and coordination. Local skills ecosystems often consider both the supply of skills available in a local economy as well as how it is deployed within emerging growth sectors. Local skills ecosystems can emerge organically and in some cases, government can play a role to providing incentives for their development. The establishment of a local skills ecosystem is often dependent on a strong anchor institution, such as a higher education or vocational education institution, strong local networks among stakeholders, as well as a catalyst for change.

Other OECD countries, such as the United States and Australia can offer key policy lessons on how to foster such an approach. Lesson from these countries include the need to involve a broad range of stakeholders, formal and informal modes of governance and cooperation, as well as local intermediaries, who are knowledgeable and entrepreneurial.

Leveraging regional intelligence to inform policy development

Understanding how local labour market needs are evolving can inform responsive policies

The development of local labour market intelligence in critical to better understand evolving needs in Northern Ireland. The Northern Ireland *Skills Barometer* is a welcome development, which provides a detailed understanding of the skill requirements for the economy up to 2026 with the aim of ensuring that any skills gaps are identified and addressed. The barometer also acts as a driver for the further development of careers education, information, advice and guidance to provide individuals with information on the current and future labour market opportunities.

Going forward, it is important for Northern Ireland to continue developing robust local labour market information on evolving skills needs to better anticipate on-going changes in the economy. Furthermore, real time labour market information is critical to inform evaluations and the development of continuous improvement mechanisms within the policy development cycle. Real time labour market information includes regular data on wages, job openings, hiring and salary trends, as well as employers who most frequently list job openings. Data production should be also supported by training on effective data utilisation to inform policy.

Examine the role of local councils in better gearing training to demand

With the increasing involvement of local councils in the skills development arena, there is a need to ensure awareness of different initiatives, sharing of best practices, and the development of a consistent quality assured approach to employer engagement. In 2013, the government introduced a reform of local government in Northern Ireland, which saw the number of local councils reduced from 26 to 11. As part of this reform, councils were awarded additional autonomies in community and local economic development. Given these new powers, local councils have an important role in reaching out to employers to understand their needs as the Councils are increasingly delivering front-line services to them. Local councils are well placed to spot emerging challenges but it is important that councils coordinate outreach with employers in a consistent, complementary and reliable manner.

Northern Ireland could consider the establishment of a Local Council Employer Engagement Group, which would be tasked with identify how to improve the overall local coordination of public services, while identifying best practices among Local Councils in engaging employers. As highlighted earlier, the local apprenticeship hub that is being implemented across several local authorities in the United Kingdom could serve as an interesting model to inform the development of such a group.

The state of training and programme implementation

Strengthen career guidance and pathways for young people

Robust career guidance plays a fundamental role in better equipping young people with information about labour market possibilities while also introducing them to practical real work experience. Strong linkages between employers and the education system are fundamental in providing appropriate feedback loops to career guidance counsellors about on-going changes in the labour market and the evolving needs of industry. The stronger engagement of employers is certainly an important component of developing a strong career guidance system.

It appears that significant progress has been made in terms of selling the benefits of apprenticeship and work-based training in Northern Ireland through Career Advisory Forums. However, more can still be done to change the mind-sets of both parents and teachers of the benefits. This can potentially be achieved by having more employers directly involved in post-primary schools providing information to students and parents about expected job opportunities and wages. Higher Level Apprenticeships in Northern Ireland in over 20 occupations will also play a critical role in promoting the use of on- and off-the-job training in high-skill jobs that will translate into positive perceptions of apprenticeship opportunities going forward.

There is an opportunity in Northern Ireland to develop more structured career pathways that provide sequential education and training programmes that offer young people "on-ramps" and "off-ramps". In an increasingly complex and fragmented labour market, career pathway models can be used to develop a balance of academic, technical, and employability skills that are well linked to an industry cluster or sector. Local education and business partnerships can be structured to provide a clear progression of courses for learners towards achieving a designated credential in a particular occupation. This type of approach can also enable secondary schools and vocational education and training providers to meet with employers to structure programming to their needs.

Within the government, there is an opportunity to improve career guidance in Northern Ireland by establishing stronger coordination between the Department for the Economy, the Department of Education, and Invest NI. A government working group could be established to examine how to strengthen the career guidance system with the goal of establishing across department strategic objectives and accountability to create policy complementarities.

Ensure a flexible training system with a focus on quality

There appears to be a good amount of flexibility in programme delivery and curriculum development within the vocational education and training system in Northern Ireland. Several programmes, such as Assured Skills and high-level apprenticeships strongly emphasise employer input into their training delivery arrangements. This does mean however that the current system tends to engage with a select number of employers. This is clearly important when resources are scare but it is also worth looking at how training can service employers operating at the "lower end" of the labour market.

Going forward, it is important that local vocational education and training programmes continue to be delivered in a flexible manner within the apprentice's normal contracted hours. This means providing greater opportunities for modular and part-time training, which balances competing demands on individuals for work and family. Modular training involves self-contained units that can be stacked against each other to complete a qualification. Part-time training involves mixing the use of evening training as well as the block release of apprenticeships for the off-the-job training portion of their framework.

Setting clear targets and goals to improve apprenticeship completion effectiveness

Northern Ireland has set a goal of increasing the number of people participating in apprenticeship programmes. This is important to frame government action. The introduction of the UK apprenticeship levy has placed new requirements on employers with a pay roll of £3 million to pay and participate in apprenticeship programmes. From a survey of employers in Northern Ireland regarding the levy, many view it as too restrictive and it appears that many are also lacking key information about their obligations under the levy scheme.

Going forward, a key issue in Northern Ireland is incentives for apprenticeship completion. Around 34% of students in apprenticeships dropped out in 2015-16, which is 1 410 out of a total of 4 130. This drop-out rate has been increasing year over year – from 32% in 2014-15 and 29% in 2013-14. Northern Ireland should examine its suite programme and services in place to encourage both apprentices and employers to complete an apprenticeship framework. Therefore, while a focus on employers is important, it is also critical to balance this interest with the needs of learners to ensure this educational pathway leads to sustainable labour market outcomes. By completing an apprenticeship, apprentices will have a transferable qualification that enables mobility and career progression.

Chapter 1. Recent economic and labour market trends in Northern Ireland

This chapter provides an overview of recent economic and labour market trends in Northern Ireland. While the 2008 economic crisis hit Northern Ireland particularly strongly, since 2015 the overall economy has seen improvements on a number of economic and employment indicators. Notably, the unemployment rate of 4.7% is very close to the UK average. Recently, Northern Ireland has introduced a new strategy to increase the number of people participating in apprenticeship programmes. Overall enrolment in apprenticeship has increased since 2012 reaching 6 500 registrations in 2016-17.

Set the context

With a population of around 1.9 million, Northern Ireland represented 2.8% of the United Kingdom's population and 2.1% of its total Gross Value Added (GVA) in 2016. Since the EU enlargement in 2004, Northern Ireland has seen increasing inflows from other European countries mainly for working reasons. The contribution of the migrant population, especially after the 2009 crises, contributed to the recovery of Northern Ireland mainly by filling low skilled occupations (Analytical Services, 2018[1]).

Key economic trends

The Northern Irish economy was gathering momentum in the mid-2000, which meant that the region was on track to catch up with other parts of the UK in terms of growth in economic activity and job creation. As shown by the trends of Gross Value Added, the impact of the 2008 global recession was felt strongly in Northern Ireland but since 2015 economic performance has become closer to that of the United Kingdom as a whole (Figure 1.1).

Figure 1.1. GVA annual growth rate, United Kingdom and Northern Ireland, 2006 – 2016

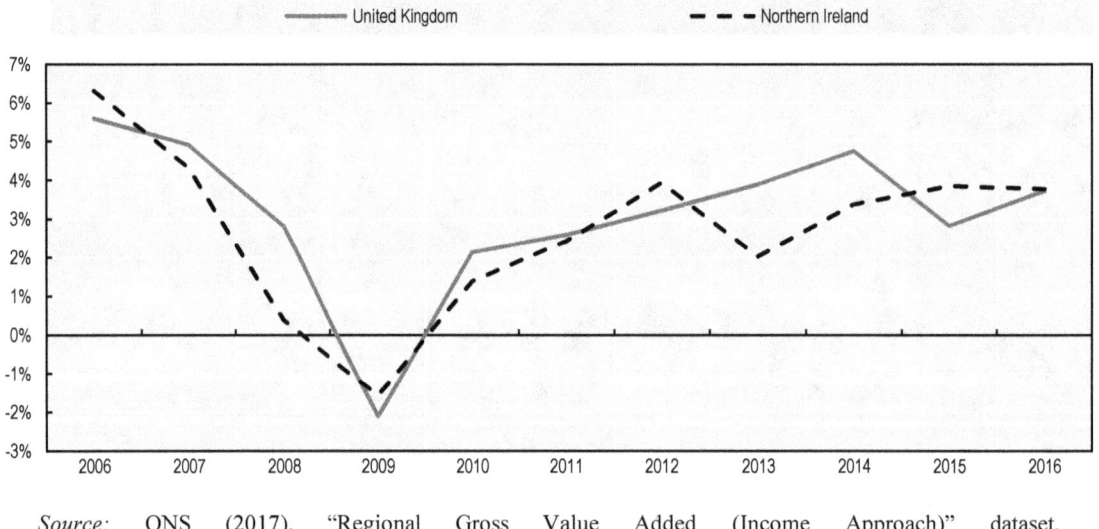

Source: ONS (2017). "Regional Gross Value Added (Income Approach)" dataset, https://www.ons.gov.uk/economy/grossvalueaddedgva/datasets/regionalgrossvalueaddedincomeapproach.

StatLink https://doi.org/10.1787/888933902947

However, recent years have been characterised by a widening gap between Northern Ireland and England and Scotland, which have the highest level of productivity measured as GVA per capita (Figure 1.2). The fact that the region of the capital city has the highest productivity in comparison to the other regions of the country is very common across OECD countries. This is mainly due to a large service sector and to their higher levels of innovation and employment creation (OECD, 2018[2]).

Within the European Union, Northern Ireland ranked 52 out of 99 NUTS1 statistical regions in 2016 in terms of Gross Domestic Product per capita; its value is similar to Walloon Region in Belgium, the East France region and the regions of Brandenburg and Thuringia in Germany.

Figure 1.2. GVA per capita, UK countries, 2006-2016

Absolute values

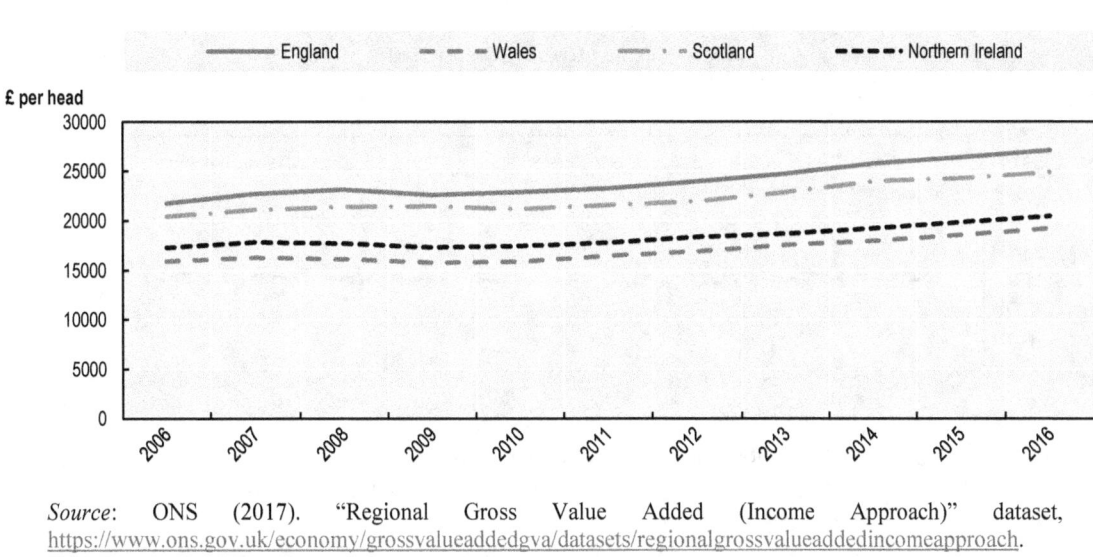

Source: ONS (2017). "Regional Gross Value Added (Income Approach)" dataset, https://www.ons.gov.uk/economy/grossvalueaddedgva/datasets/regionalgrossvalueaddedincomeapproach.

StatLink https://doi.org/10.1787/888933902966

The level of GVA per capita is relatively similar across sub-regions of Northern Ireland, with the exception of Belfast whose GVA per capita is double that of any other sub-regions (Figure 1.3). Between 2000-15, the growth in GVA per capita has also not been evenly distributed throughout the region, with Belfast having experienced the strongest growth, thus pulling even further ahead compared to other parts of Northern Ireland.

A recent report also highlights the great potential of Belfast in the next decade. The capital of Northern Ireland could become the second fastest-growing financial services centre in the UK, growing by around 25% by 2025. The advantages of Belfast are the presence of a skilled workforce, easy access to London and strong collaboration with both Queen's University and Invest NI. The proximity to the Republic of Ireland will also be an asset after the Brexit (TheCityUK, 2017[3]).

Figure 1.3. GVA per capita, sub-regions of Northern Ireland, 2006-2016

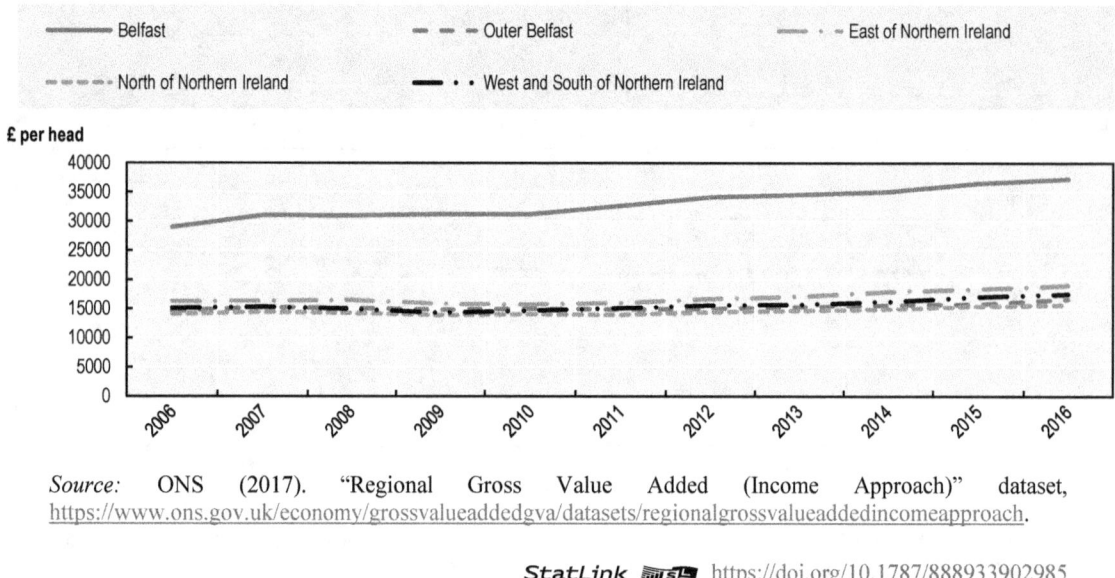

Source: ONS (2017). "Regional Gross Value Added (Income Approach)" dataset, https://www.ons.gov.uk/economy/grossvalueaddedgva/datasets/regionalgrossvalueaddedincomeapproach.

StatLink https://doi.org/10.1787/888933902985

Figure 1.4. GVA per capita annual growth rate, sub-regions of Northern Ireland, 2000-2016

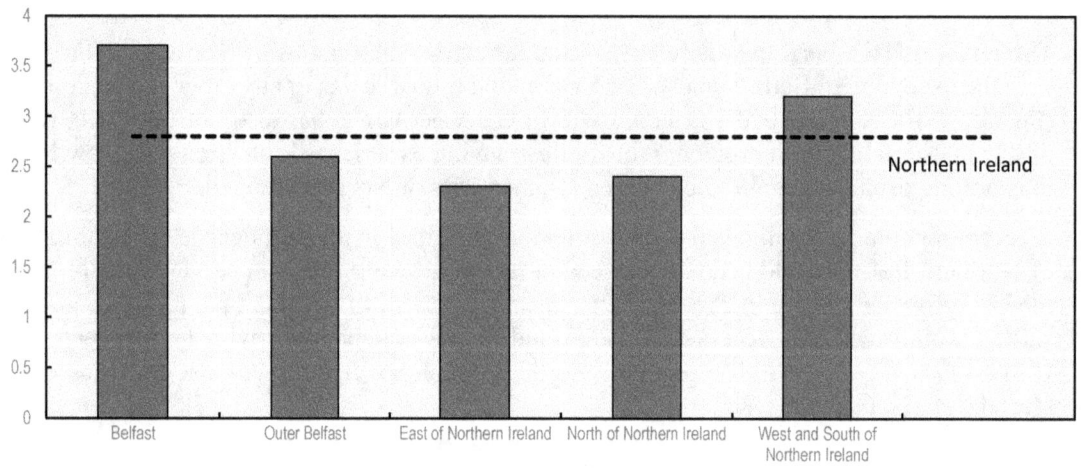

Source: ONS (2017). "Regional Gross Value Added (Income Approach)" dataset, https://www.ons.gov.uk/economy/grossvalueaddedgva/datasets/regionalgrossvalueaddedincomeapproach.

StatLink https://doi.org/10.1787/888933903004

Figure 1.5 shows that, labour productivity, approximated by the Gross Value Added per filled job, is relatively low in Northern Ireland in comparison with England and Scotland. This explains part of the gap in income between Northern Ireland and the rest of UK, and affects most sectors with the exception of manufacturing and public services for which Northern Ireland performs relatively well (Johnston and Buchanan, 2016[4]) (Flynn, 2016[5]). Within Northern Ireland, the East region as well as Belfast and Outer Belfast contribute more substantially to productivity growth.

Figure 1.5. Gross Value Added per filled job, 2016

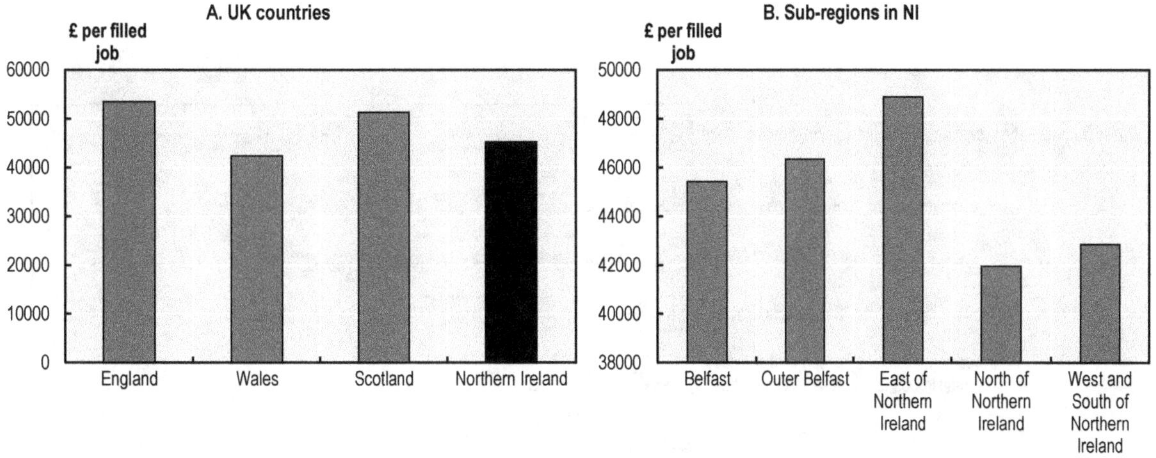

Source: ONS (2017). "Sub-regional Productivity: Labour Productivity (GVA per hour worked and GVA per filled job) indices by UK NUTS2 and NUTS3 sub-regions" dataset, https://www.ons.gov.uk/employmentandlabourmarket/peopleinwork/labourproductivity/datasets/subregionalproductivitylabourproductivitygvaperhourworkedandgvaperfilledjobindicesbyuknuts2andnuts3subregions.

StatLink https://doi.org/10.1787/888933903023

Looking at the share of GVA by industry within Northern Ireland, Figure 1.6 shows that public administration, social services, education and human health contribute a significant proportion to overall GVA within Northern Ireland. This speaks to the importance of the public sector within Northern Ireland, which drives many employment and economic development opportunities. Comparing Northern Ireland to the UK average, this share of public administration activity is much higher. Professionals, scientific, and technical activities are behind the UK average, which should be a source of attention within Northern Ireland because of their overall contribution to productivity and innovation.

Figure 1.6. Share of total GVA by industry at current basic prices, United Kingdom and Northern Ireland, 2015

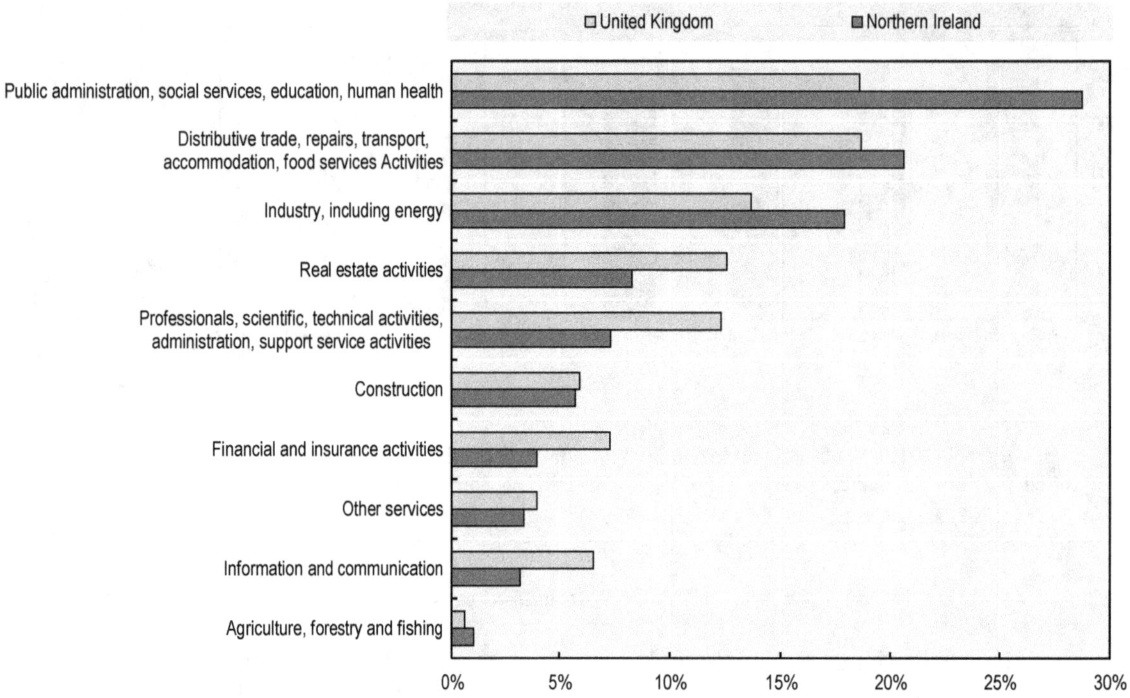

Source: OECD calculations based on OECD (2018), OECD Regional Statistics (database), http://dx.doi.org/10.1787/region-data-en.

StatLink https://doi.org/10.1787/888933903042

Labour market trends

The number of people in employment increased by 36 000 people between 2008 and 2016. This change is mainly due to the increasing inward migration from European countries which reached rose by 40 000 people over the same period. While in other UK regions, migrants from inside and outside the European Union are evenly distributed, in Northern Ireland more than 70% of migrants are from another European country. The top countries of origin are the Republic of Ireland, Poland and Lithuania (Analytical Services, 2018[1]).

Figure 1.7. People in employment by country of birth in Northern Ireland, 2008 and 2016

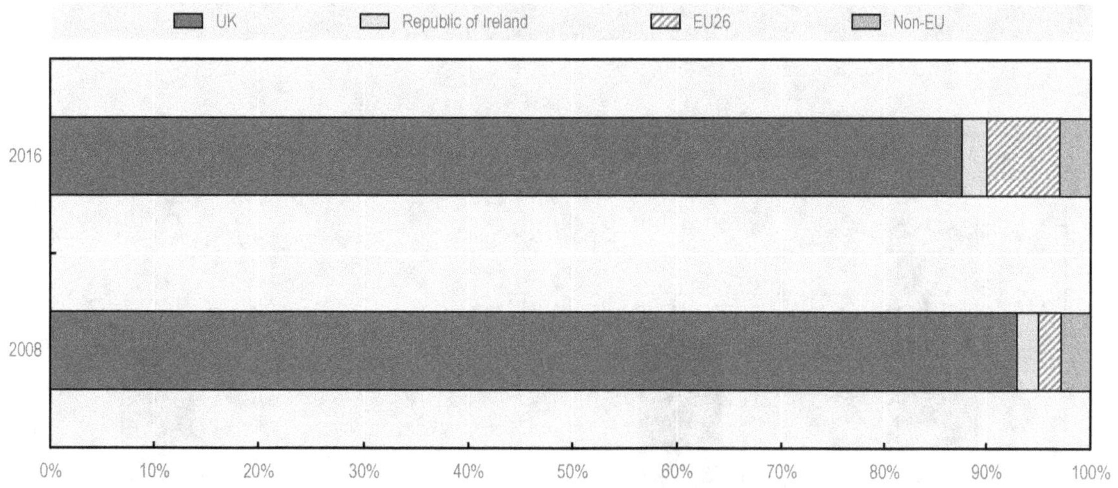

Source: NISRA (2018), Labour Force Survey

StatLink ᵐˢᵖ https://doi.org/10.1787/888933903061

Box 1.1. Impact of Brexit on the Northern Irish labour market

The exit from the European Union poses a number of challenges for the Northern Irish labour market which relies heavily on foreign workers in a number of economic sectors. According to the Labour Force Survey (LFS) data, EU27 migrants represent more than 6% of the Northern Ireland population and 9% of its workforce. Among them, more than 70% are from an EU country excluding the Republic of Ireland.

Migrants in Northern Ireland are concentrated in a number of economic sectors including manufacturing, health and social care, hospitality and elementary occupations. EU migrants tend to work primarily in lower skilled occupations in the agri-food sector.

Employers in Northern Ireland have expressed their concerns in relation to the access to foreign workers especially in sectors heavily relying on the migrant population and on their ability to retain them in the region. In addition to the skills shortages deriving from Brexit, concerns exist in relation to the exchange of goods across the border between Northern Ireland and the Republic of Ireland that currently pass the border without checks.

As Northern Ireland accounts for between 10 and 12% of total exports from Ireland to the UK and accounted for 7 to 8% of imports, the existence of a border between the two countries would affect many different supply chains.

Source: (The Expert Group on Future Skills Needs, 2018[6])

Looking at labour market trends in Northern Ireland, the employment rate in 2016 was lower than in the rest of the United Kingdom but higher than the EU-28. Values are close to the OECD average (Figure 1.8). While in the United Kingdom the employment rate has increased in the last decade, in Northern Ireland and in the EU-28 has been stable over time.

Figure 1.8. Employment rate, United Kingdom, Northern Ireland, EU-28 and OECD, 2006 and 2016

Population 15 and above

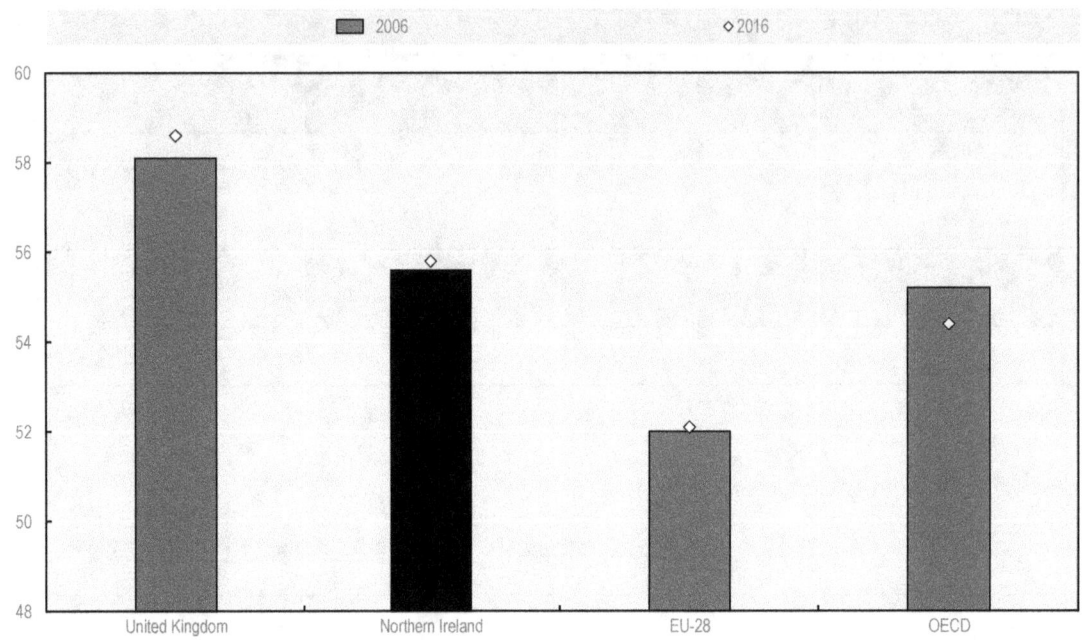

Note: Data for the OECD refers to years 2006 and 2014.
Source: OECD (2018), OECD Regional Statistics (database), http://dx.doi.org/10.1787/region-data-en.

StatLink https://doi.org/10.1787/888933903080

As shown in Figure 1.9, significant differences exist across Northern Irish sub-regions, with Derry City and Strabane having an employment rate of 46.4% rising to 62.5% in Lisburn and Castlereagh. The low employment of Derry City and Strabane is part of a broader set of indicators highlighting the overall deprivation and difficult labour market condition of the district. More precisely, it also has the highest claimant count rate (at 5.3% of the population 16-64) and very high shares of people with no qualification compared to the rest of the United Kingdom (Northern Ireland Statistics and Research Agency,(n.d.)[7])

Figure 1.9. Employment rate, Northern Irish LGDs, 2016

Population 16 and above

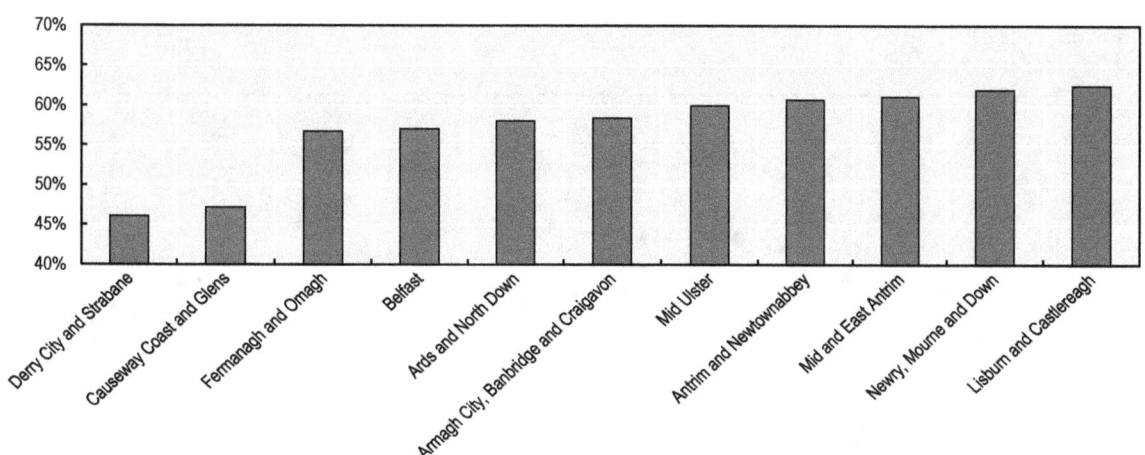

Source: NISRA (2017). 'Labour Force Survey Tables for Local Government Districts 2016', https://www.nisra.gov.uk/publications/labour-force-survey-tables-local-government-districts-2016.

StatLink https://doi.org/10.1787/888933903099

Labour market trends show that employment changes in Northern Ireland have significantly fluctuated over the last 15 years. Following a deep fall in employment between 2005 and 2008, the recovery has been precarious, with employment growth being halted in 2012 and 2013 before starting to rise. At 4.7% in 2017, the unemployment rate in Northern Ireland is relatively low compared to other OECD economies and sits just above the UK average (Figure 1.10). While the overall unemployment rate is slightly above the UK average, Figure 1.11 displays a favourable youth unemployment rate of 10% in 2017 which sits below the UK average. Youth unemployment has improved significantly since its peak rate of 22% in 2013.

Figure 1.10. Unemployment rate, selected European countries, 2007-2017

Population 15-64

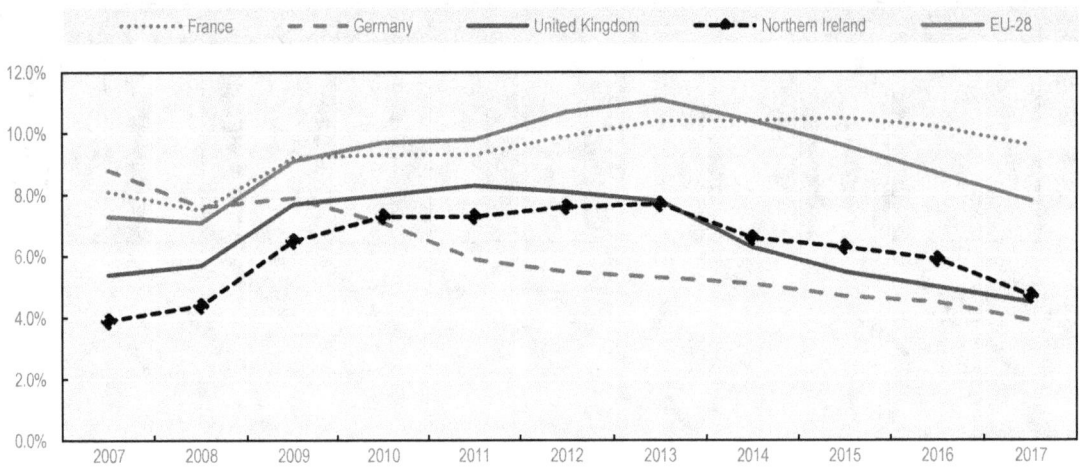

Source: OECD (2018), OECD Regional Statistics (database), http://dx.doi.org/10.1787/region-data-en.

StatLink https://doi.org/10.1787/888933903118

Figure 1.11. Youth unemployment rate, selected European countries, 2007-2017

Population 15-24

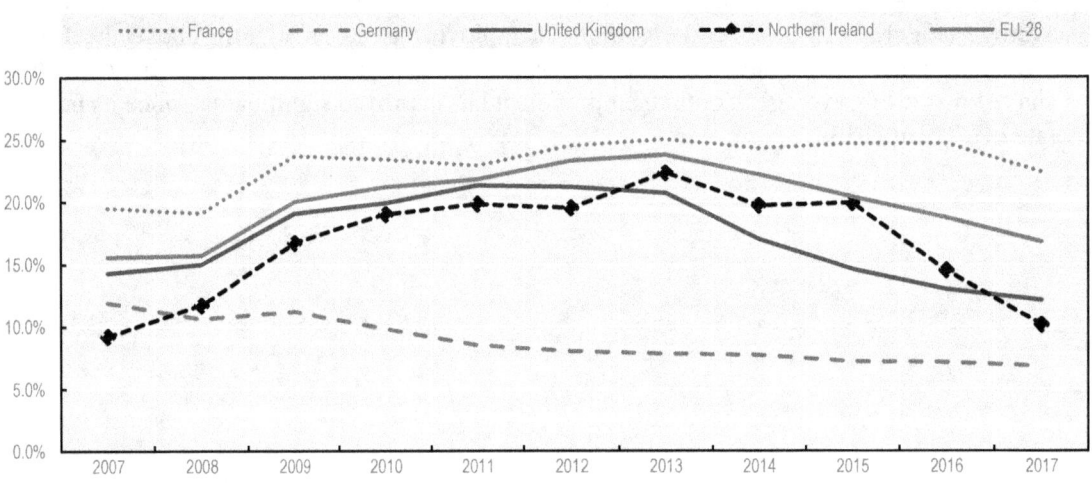

Source: OECD (2018), OECD Regional Statistics (database), http://dx.doi.org/10.1787/region-data-en.

StatLink https://doi.org/10.1787/888933903137

While the labour market has recovered relatively well after the economic crisis, the long-term unemployment rate (share of unemployed people looking for a job for more than 12 months) and the high economic inactivity remain the two main challenges for the Northern Irish economy. Between the recent economic crisis and 2015, long-term unemployment rate has increased in Northern Ireland. While it has slightly decreased in recent years, it is still significantly higher that the UK average (Figure 1.12). Being in unemployment for a long time can make it harder for people to go back to employment and can have an economic impact both for individuals and for the country as a whole (OECD, 2011[8]).

Recent data also shows that inactivity rate was quite steady between 2011 and 2015 but is increasing again since 2017 (Figure 1.13). The gap with the rest of the UK is related to a number of factors characterising Northern Ireland such as high inactivity for people with children, the increasing number of people with mental health problems as well as the number of students (Ulster University Economic Policy Centre, 2016[9]).

Figure 1.12. Long-term unemployment rate, selected European countries, 2007-2017

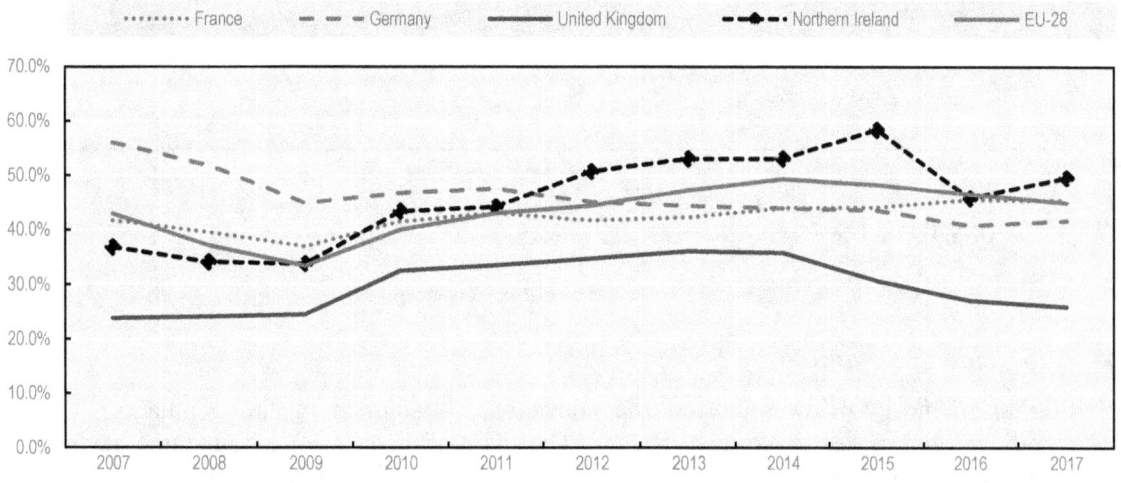

Note: Long-term unemployment refers to people who have been unemployed for more than 12 months. The figure shows long-term unemployment as the share of total unemployment.
Source: Eurostat Regional Labour Market Statistics.

StatLink https://doi.org/10.1787/888933903156

Figure 1.13. Economic inactivity rate, UK countries, 2007-2017

Share of people aged 16-64 who are not in the labour force

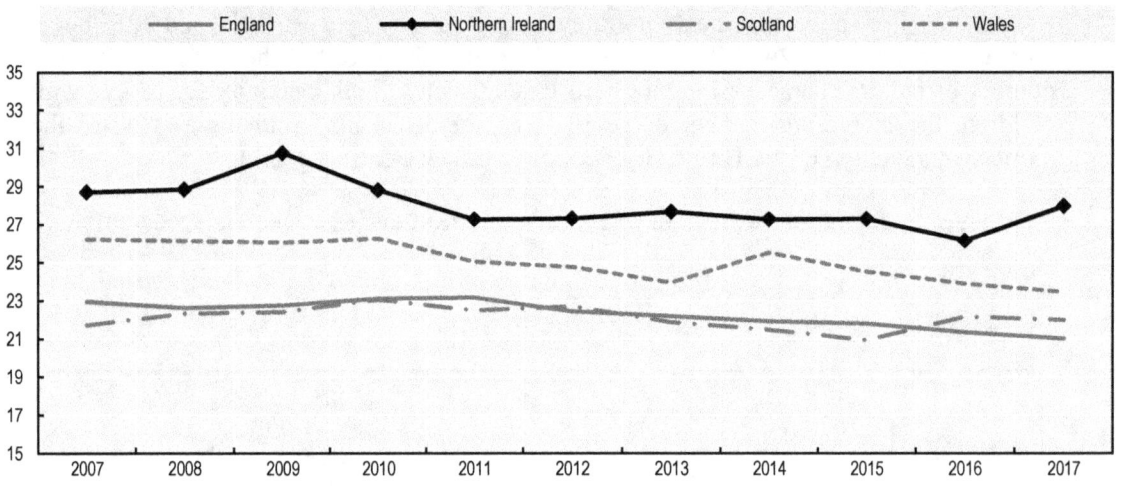

Source: ONS, Labour Force Survey

StatLink https://doi.org/10.1787/888933903175

Education and training

Similar to most OECD countries, the educational attainment of the population has significantly increased in Northern Ireland. The share of those in the labour force having achieved tertiary education was 38.4% in 2017, up from 30.2% in 2007. Yet the share of the labour force having only achieved primary education is higher compared to the UK average (20.9% in NI vs. 16.7% in the UK) (see Figure 1.14). As shown in Figure 1.15, there are major sub-regional differences in the education attainment of the working age population, especially in the share of people with no education, ranging between 9.7% in Lisburn and Castlereagh to 22.1% in Newry, Mourne and Down.

Figure 1.14. Share of the labour force by educational attainment, United Kingdom and Northern Ireland, 2007 and 2017

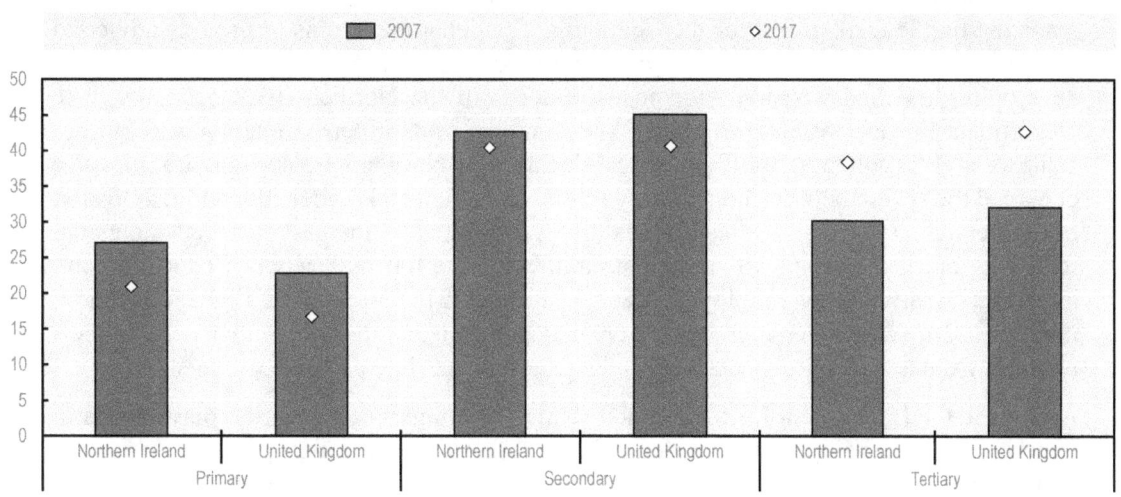

Source: OECD (2018), OECD Regional Statistics (database), http://dx.doi.org/10.1787/region-data-en.

StatLink https://doi.org/10.1787/888933903194

Figure 1.15. Share of the population aged 15-64 by educational attainment, Northern Irish LGDs, 2016

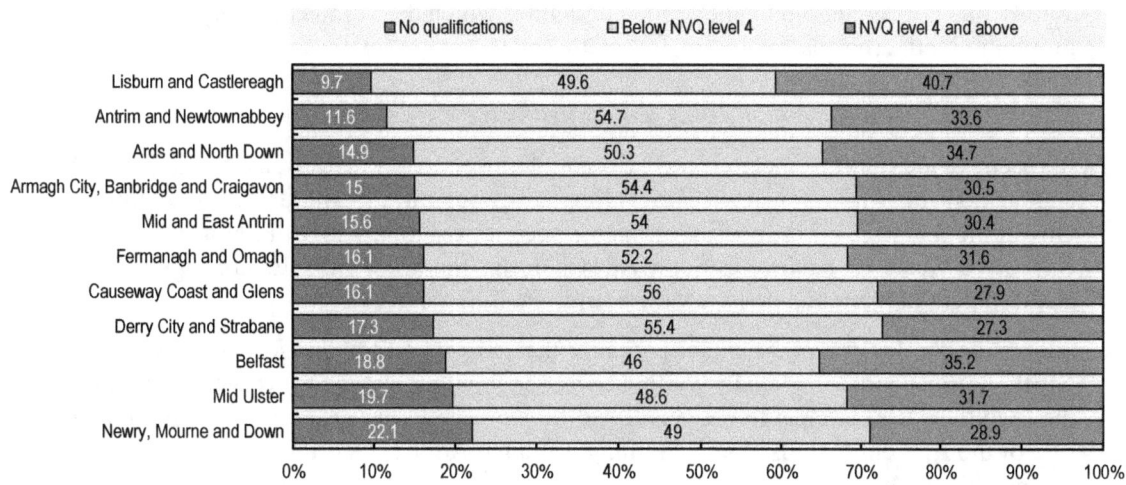

Source: NISRA (2018). 'Labour Force Survey Tables for Local Government Districts 2017', https://www.nisra.gov.uk/publications/labour-force-survey-tables-local-government-districts-2017.

StatLink https://doi.org/10.1787/888933903213

Key government departments implementing employment and skills policies

Employment and skills programmes (including apprenticeships) in Northern Ireland are managed by the Department for the Economy. The department aims to provide advice to job seekers and employers on employment and recruitment programmes with the goal of developing a skilled workforce to meet the needs of the Northern Irish economy. The Department is responsible for policy and funding of Northern Ireland's six Further Education (FE) colleges. While Further Education in Northern Ireland has traditionally occupied the sphere between compulsory school education and higher education, delivered by universities (OECD, 2014[10]), it has also contributed to increasing social inclusion, removing barriers to employment and strengthening the linkages between education and industry (Department for Employment and Learning, 2016). In terms of higher education, there are also two universities, which are independent private bodies that receive their incomes from a number of sources, including student fees but also public funds.

Alongside the Department for the Economy, the Department of Education plays a role in fostering skills development opportunities by developing the capacity of the education sector and ensuring quality education standards. The Department of Education is responsible for curriculum and learning development as well as ensuring the infrastructure of schools across Northern Ireland.

Invest NI, Northern Ireland's business development agency, works closely with employers in Northern Ireland to help them identify and articulate current and future skills needs ((Invest Northern Ireland,(n.d.)[11]). Invest NI supports companies which are exporting or planning to export and promotes inward investments in the region. Collectively, they employ over 100,000 people and deliver £16bn annually of sales outside Northern Ireland. Within this is a core group of about 900 companies which deliver the majority of economic growth in Northern Ireland.

Recent government reforms and policy initiatives

In recent years, significant efforts have been undertaken in Northern Ireland to improve the engagement of employers in skills development programmes. The draft Programme for Government (2016-2021) focuses on major societal outcomes that the Northern Ireland Executive wants to achieve and provides a basis for all sectors to contribute to the development of plans and actions (Northern Ireland Executive, 2016[12])

Alongside the Programme for Government, the Industrial Strategy sets out a vision for Northern Ireland to be a globally competitive economy that works for everyone, embracing the twin themes of competitiveness and well-being. The Industrial Strategy highlights the role of the Apprenticeships/Youth Training Strategic Advisory Forum (SAF) and Sectoral Partnerships in bringing employers, further education colleges, the universities and other key stakeholders together to ensure provision meets the needs of employers and the wider economy (Department for the Economy, 2016[13]). The SAF is an interim forum until a new Minister is in place to make the appointments to a permanent Forum.

Sectoral Partnerships (SPs) are led by employers who are knowledgeable about the skills needs of their sector. Current sectors include Hospitality and Events, Manufacturing and Engineering, ICT, Finance and Accounting, Life Sciences and the Built Environment By 2021, there are plans for a further 11 sectoral partnerships to be developed.

Northern Ireland strategy on apprenticeship

The Northern Ireland strategy on apprenticeships, Securing our Success, released in 2014 focused on transforming the skills landscape to ensure the Northern Ireland economy has the skills needed to grow and compete globally (Department for Employment and Learning, 2014[14]). ApprenticeshipsNI 2017 is an apprenticeship model designed to engage with businesses and respond directly to their needs in terms of ease of access, relevant training, incentives and support (Department for the Economy, 2018[15]) (see box).

Box 1.2. ApprenticeshipsNI

Under ApprenticeshipsNI 2017, apprenticeships are open to all people who have reached the minimum school leaving age, and who meet the entry requirements set out in the relevant apprenticeships framework. Under this model, apprenticeships usually take at least two years and up to four years to complete although, unlike traditional apprenticeships, are not time-served. Programmes are designed to enable mobility within a sector and across the wider economy by including a breadth of training beyond the specific needs of a job through both on and off-the-job training.

The key elements of ApprenticeshipsNI 2017 are permanent remunerative employment for the apprentice from day one with a minimum of 21 contracted hours per week with one employer, which includes day release / off-the-job training (directed training must be paid as part of the apprentice's contracted hours). Payment to the apprentice of a wage commensurate with the industry rate for that job and in accordance with the National Minimum Wage (NMW) regulations. An apprenticeship framework for the specific occupational area agreed with the relevant industry-led representative body, comprising directed training, related knowledge, appropriate Essential Skills, and structured workplace training. A Personal Training Plan (PTP) that is discussed and agreed between the Contractor, the employer, and the apprentice detailing the progression route for achieving the agreed qualifications

---

Young people are eligible to enter ApprenticeshipsNI 2017 provided they fulfil the eligibility criteria. For those apprentices aged under 25 years at the time of programme registration, the full costs of the 'off-the-job' training for the duration of the apprenticeship will be paid.

Support for adult apprenticeships is targeted to the economically important sectors needed to rebalance the economy. In addition, adult apprentices must fulfil the eligibility criteria. Half of the funding will be paid in respect of those aged 25 years and over for the duration of their apprenticeship in the following sectors: Advanced Engineering (including Construction Technical); Advanced Manufacturing; Business Services (Specifically ICT); Creative Industries; Financial Services; Food and Drink Manufacturing; and Life and Health Sciences.

Training suppliers must conduct an initial assessment of each apprentice in order to determine the level of their existing skills and competences in general. The purpose of this initial assessment is to identify each apprentice's strengths and weaknesses, professional and technical training, and Essential Skills, as well as to assess which level of the programme is most appropriate to meet their needs.

Departmental provision includes a central service to assist the growth of apprenticeships, a strategic advisory forum and a series of sectoral partnerships to facilitate stakeholder engagement, and a revised Careers system to ensure that individuals are fully aware of the range of apprenticeship opportunities and pathways (Department for the Economy, 2018[15])

The model is focused on employer-led training provision with employers creating apprenticeships in line with business needs (Department for the Economy, 2017[16]). The central service supports businesses participation, particularly SMEs and participants, and includes an online portal called Connect to Success for advertising apprenticeship opportunities. The introduction of the Skills Barometer supports the better matching of the supply and demand of apprentices by providing a clear indication of current, emerging and long term skills shortages.

These mechanisms are all new developments within Northern Ireland. Central services enables employers to put their vacancies online. Apprentices are also able to their CVs online to facilitated matching. The Department recognise the need to support businesses to understand how to recruit apprentices. They offer a one-to-one service, effectively a peripatetic role where someone goes in and helps business to design on the job training so it matches the training provided off the job. This is an evolving system given that it is relatively new.

Apprenticeship participation rates

In a number of OECD countries, there is a long tradition of apprenticeships. As shown in Figure 1.16 below, countries such as Germany and Austria have a take-up rate above 30% and Denmark, the Netherland and Australia between 15% and 19%. In Northern Ireland take up rate is around 5%, slightly above the value for England.

Figure 1.16. Use of apprenticeships across OECD countries, 2015

Current apprentices in programmes leading to upper-secondary or shorter post-secondary qualifications as a share of all students enrolled in upper-secondary and shorter post-secondary education (ISCED 3 and ISCED 4C), 16-65-year-olds (2012)

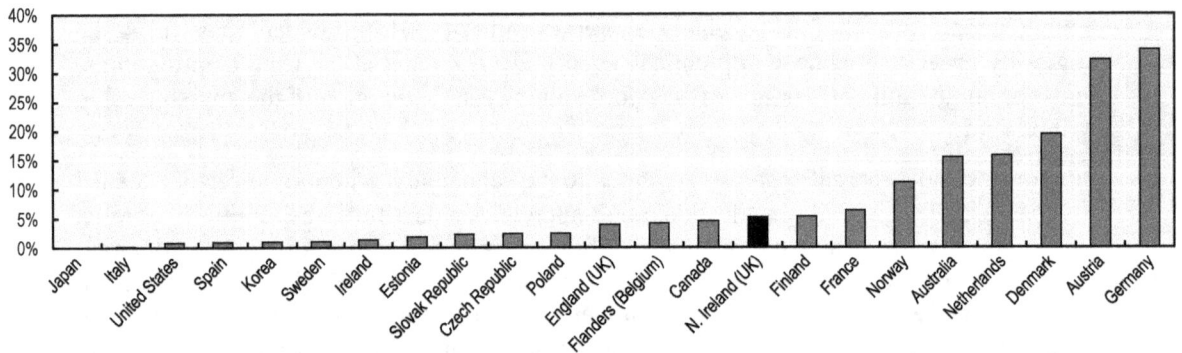

Note: The data are based on self-report and may therefore undercount apprentices in England given evidence that some of them are not aware that they are apprentices. In Japan, Italy, the United States, Spain, Sweden, Korea and Ireland the estimated share of current apprentices is not significantly different from zero.
Source: OECD (2016), Survey of Adult Skills (PIAAC) (Database 2012, 2015), www.oecd.org/skills/piaac/publicdataandanalysis/.

StatLink https://doi.org/10.1787/888933903232

In Northern Ireland the total number of participants in apprenticeship programmes starting at all levels has moved from 5 202 in the academic year 2013/14 to 6 499 in 2016/17. The vast majority of apprentices are aged 16-24 and even if the share of apprentices aged 25 and above has increased in recent years, it represented 16.2% of total apprentices in 2016/2017. Around 60% of apprentices are men and the share of women has slightly decreased in recent years from 41% in the academic year 2013/ 2014 to 38% in 2016/2017.

Figure 1.17. ApprenticeshipsNI starts by age groups, 2013-2017

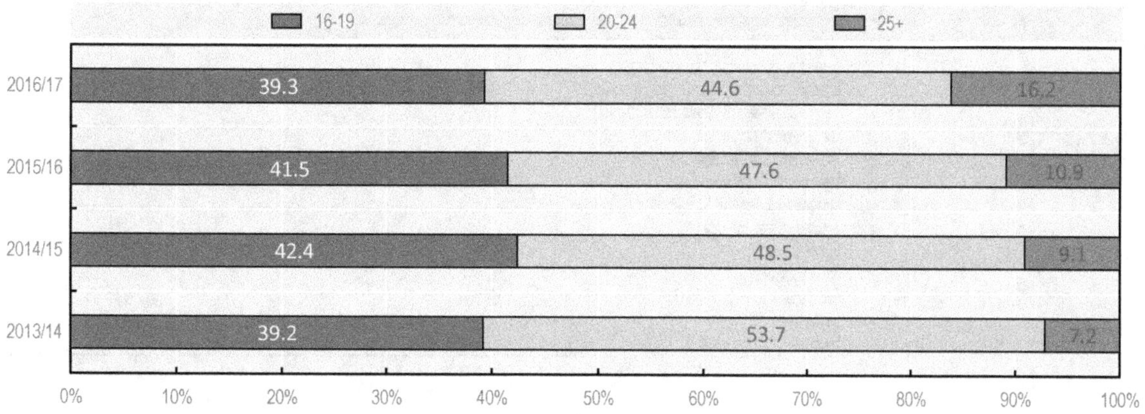

Year	16-19	20-24	25+
2016/17	39.3	44.6	16.2
2015/16	41.5	47.6	10.9
2014/15	42.4	48.5	9.1
2013/14	39.2	53.7	7.2

Source: Northern Ireland Statistics and Research Agency (2018). "ApprenticeshipsNI Statistical Bulletin, 2018" https://www.economy-ni.gov.uk/articles/apprenticeshipsni-statistics.

StatLink https://doi.org/10.1787/888933903251

Figure 1.18. ApprenticeshipsNI starts by gender, 2013-2017

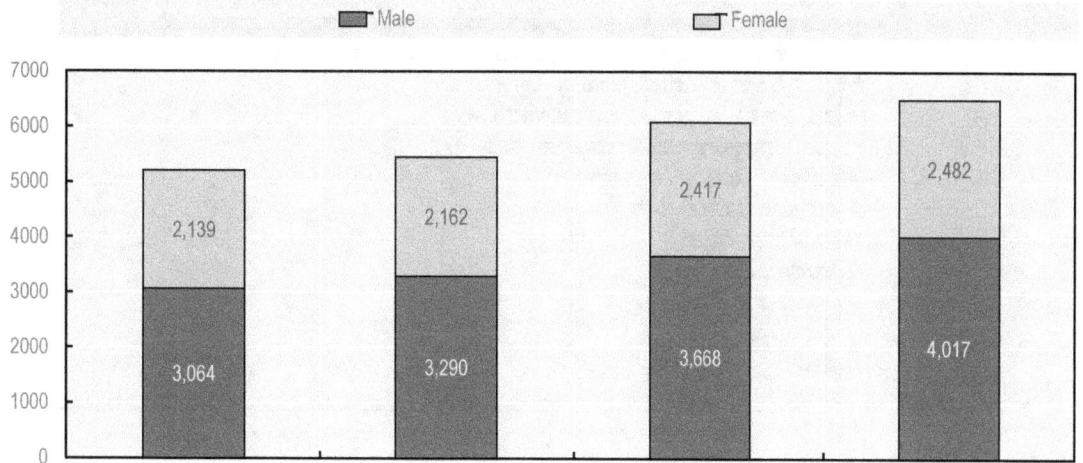

Source: Northern Ireland Statistics and Research Agency (2018). "ApprenticeshipsNI Statistical Bulletin, 2018" https://www.economy-ni.gov.uk/articles/apprenticeshipsni-statistics.

StatLink https://doi.org/10.1787/888933903270

While for both genders the majority of apprenticeships have NVQ levels 2, the field of training is very different, with men participating mainly in Electrotechnical, Engineering and vehicle maintenance and Repair frameworks (figure 1.19) and women in Health and Social care, Hospitality and Food manufacture (figure 1.20). Food manufacture, Hospitality and Retail are the only fields of training which are common to both genders.

Figure 1.19. Main fields of training for men, 2013-2017

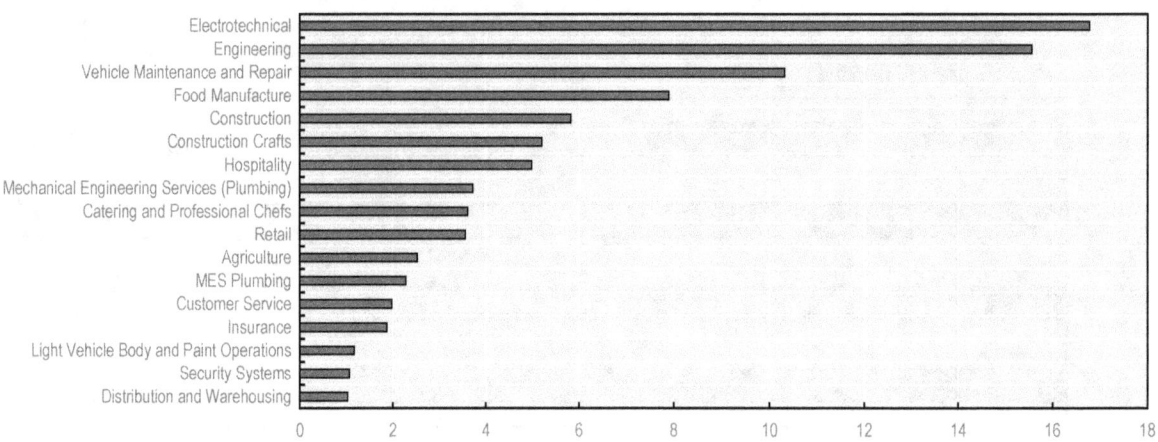

Source: Northern Ireland Statistics and Research Agency (2018). "ApprenticeshipsNI Statistical Bulletin, 2018" https://www.economy-ni.gov.uk/articles/apprenticeshipsni-statistics.

StatLink https://doi.org/10.1787/888933903289

Figure 1.20. Main fields of training for women, 2013-2017

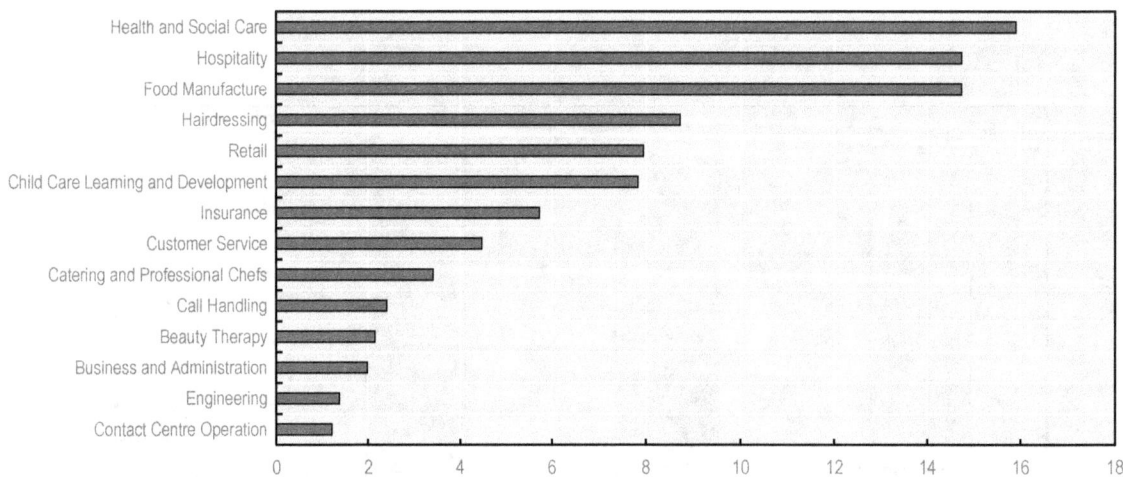

Source: Northern Ireland Statistics and Research Agency (2018). "ApprenticeshipsNI Statistical Bulletin, 2018" https://www.economy-ni.gov.uk/articles/apprenticeshipsni-statistics.

StatLink https://doi.org/10.1787/888933903308

Since the beginning of ApprenticeshipsNI in 2013, 19 942 participants left the programme and among them around 60% achieved their targeted Full Framework. In 2016/2017, the share of leavers at Level 2 achieving a Full Framework was 65% compared to 33% in 2013/2014. The increase is even stronger for leaver at Level 3 for which the share of leavers achieving a full framework was 61% compared to 19% in 2013/2014.

Figure 1.21 shows the distribution of participants by Local Government Districts in the region. While Belfast has the highest number of participants on ApprenticeshipsNI 2013 and ApprenticeshipsNI 2017, for the other Local Government Districts the number of participants does not seem to be related to the population size.

Figure 1.21. Number of participants on ApprenticeshipsNI 2013 and ApprenticeshipsNI 2017 by Local Government District

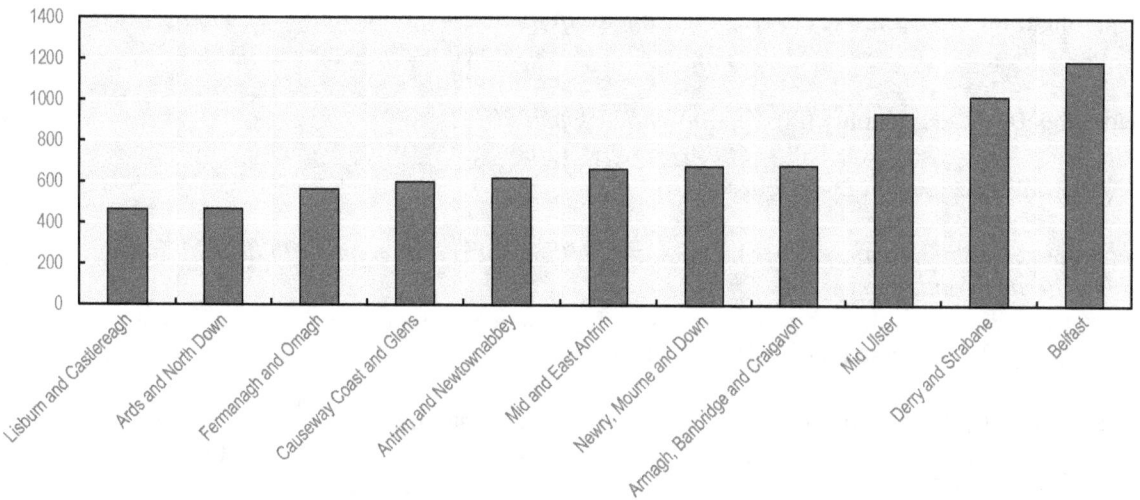

Note These figures are for apprentices on ApprenticeshipsNI, they do not include those apprentices who remain on the Jobskills Modern Apprenticeships programme.
Source: Northern Ireland Statistics and Research Agency (2018). "ApprenticeshipsNI Statistical Bulletin, 2018" https://www.economy-ni.gov.uk/articles/apprenticeshipsni-statistics.

StatLink https://doi.org/10.1787/888933903327

Conclusions

Northern Ireland has made positive progress on a range of employment, and economic indicators. The economy is characterised by a high share of employment in the public sector, which provide a stable foundation for future economic activity. While the unemployment rate compares favourably with the UK, youth unemployment and economic inactivity remain key challenges going forward.

This is where apprenticeship opportunities will play an important role in boosting overall school to work transitions. Northern Ireland has recently introduced a new apprenticeship strategy and strong efforts have been made to increase overall participation in this educational pathway. Employers will be critical partners to boost overall private sector employment and ensure that more apprenticeship programmes can be developed in new and emerging sectors of the economy such as information and communications technology.

References

Analytical Services, D. (2018), "Northern Ireland migration, labour and skills", https://www.economy-ni.gov.uk/sites/default/files/publications/economy/Northern-Ireland-migration-labour-and-skills-Final.pdf (accessed on 23 October 2018). [1]

Department for Employment and Learning (2014), *Securing our Success: The Northern Ireland Strategy on Apprenticeships*, https://www.economy-ni.gov.uk/sites/default/files/publications/del/Securing%20our%20Success%20The%20NI%20Strategy%20on%20Apprenticeships.pdf (accessed on 25 October 2018). [14]

Department for the Economy (2018), *Apprenticeship guidelines*, https://www.economy-ni.gov.uk/publications/apprenticeship-guidelines (accessed on 26 October 2018). [15]

Department for the Economy (2017), *ApprenticeshipNI 2017*, http://www.apprenticeshipalliances.eu/wp-content/uploads/2018/05/Apprenticeships-NI-2017.pdf (accessed on 26 October 2018). [16]

Department for the Economy (2016), *Economy 2030: A consultation on an Industrial Strategy for Northern Ireland*, https://www.economy-ni.gov.uk/sites/default/files/consultations/economy/industrial-strategy-ni-consultation-document.pdf (accessed on 25 October 2018). [13]

Flynn, P. (2016), "Productivity and the Northern Ireland Economy", https://www.nerinstitute.net/download/pdf/industrial_policy_wp_2016_061216.pdf (accessed on 26 October 2018). [5]

Invest Northern Ireland((n.d.)), *InvestNI*, https://www.investni.com/news/index.html (accessed on 26 October 2018). [11]

Johnston, R. and J. Buchanan (2016), *Understanding productivity in Northern Ireland*, https://www.ulster.ac.uk/__data/assets/pdf_file/0008/118385/Understanding_productivity_in_Northern_Ireland_27_September_2016.pdf (accessed on 26 October 2018). [4]

Northern Ireland Executive (2016), *Draft Programme for Government Framework 2016-2021*, https://www.northernireland.gov.uk/sites/default/files/consultations/newnigov/draft-pfg-framework-2016-21.pdf (accessed on 26 October 2018). [12]

Northern Ireland Statistics and Research Agency((n.d.)), *Labour Force Survey*, https://www.nisra.gov.uk/statistics/labour-market-and-social-welfare/labour-force-survey (accessed on 26 October 2018). [7]

OECD (2018), *OECD Regions and Cities at a Glance 2018*, OECD Publishing, Paris, http://dx.doi.org/10.1787/reg_cit_glance-2018-en. [2]

OECD (2014), *Employment and Skills Strategies in Northern Ireland, United Kingdom*, OECD Reviews on Local Job Creation, OECD Publishing, Paris, http://dx.doi.org/10.1787/9789264208872-en. [10]

OECD (2011), *OECD Economic Outlook, Volume 2011 Issue 1*, OECD Publishing, Paris, http://dx.doi.org/10.1787/eco_outlook-v2011-1-en. [8]

The Expert Group on Future Skills Needs (2018), *Addressing the Skills Needs Arising from the Potential Trade Implications of Brexit*, https://dbei.gov.ie/en/Publications/Publication-files/Skills-needs-potential-trade-implications-Brexit.pdf (accessed on 23 October 2018). [6]

TheCityUK (2017), *A vision for a transformed, world-leading industry: UK-based financial and related professional services*, https://www.pwc.co.uk/who-we-are/regions/northernireland/CityUK-FutureOfFS_060717.pdf (accessed on 25 October 2018). [3]

Ulster University Economic Policy Centre (2016), "An anatomy of economic inactivity in Northern Ireland", https://www.ulster.ac.uk/__data/assets/pdf_file/0004/181435/UUEPC-Inactivity-Discussion-Paper-Final-Report.pdf (accessed on 25 October 2018). [9]

Chapter 2. Understanding firm dynamics and skills in Northern Ireland

This chapter presents findings from the OECD employer survey that was conducted in Northern Ireland. Based on responses received from 127 employers, the results provide useful insights on employers experience with apprenticeship programmes as well as their barriers to training. In addition, it provides information on employers' perception of the Apprenticeship Levy scheme and its implementation in Northern Ireland.

The profile of Northern Irish firms

Similar to many other European countries, nearly all companies in Northern Ireland can be classified as small and medium-size (SME) enterprises as defined by the European Commission (EC). More precisely, 88% of firms in Northern Ireland have less than 10 employees, and 9.4% have between 10 and 49 employees (NISRA, 2018[17]).

In 2015, 850 businesses in Northern Ireland were owned by a company based abroad. These companies employed just under 100 000 workers, representing around 13% of total employment. The number of foreign-owned businesses has grown by 33% between 2008 and 2015, with associated employment increasing by 41% over the same period. The Republic of Ireland accounts for the largest share of foreign-owned businesses (290), whilst companies based in the United States had the largest contribution to total employment in Northern Ireland with 24 000 employees (Northern Ireland Assembly, 2016[18])

The industrial composition of Northern Irish enterprises presents some differences from the United Kingdom (UK) average, which can be seen in Figure 2.1. In particular there is a higher share of firms operating in the primary sector and utilities (14.6% vs. 5.9%), in the wholesale and retail sector (21.3% vs. 19.9%) and in the education sector (5.6% vs. 3.1%). In contrast, the United Kingdom has higher shares of firms operating in business services (22.2% vs. 12.0%), in information and communication (4.5% vs. 1.7%) and in hotels and restaurants (9.2% vs. 7.4%). These structures could have an impact on the quality of employment and the economic growth of the country.

Figure 2.1. Sectoral composition of firms, United Kingdom and Northern Ireland, 2017

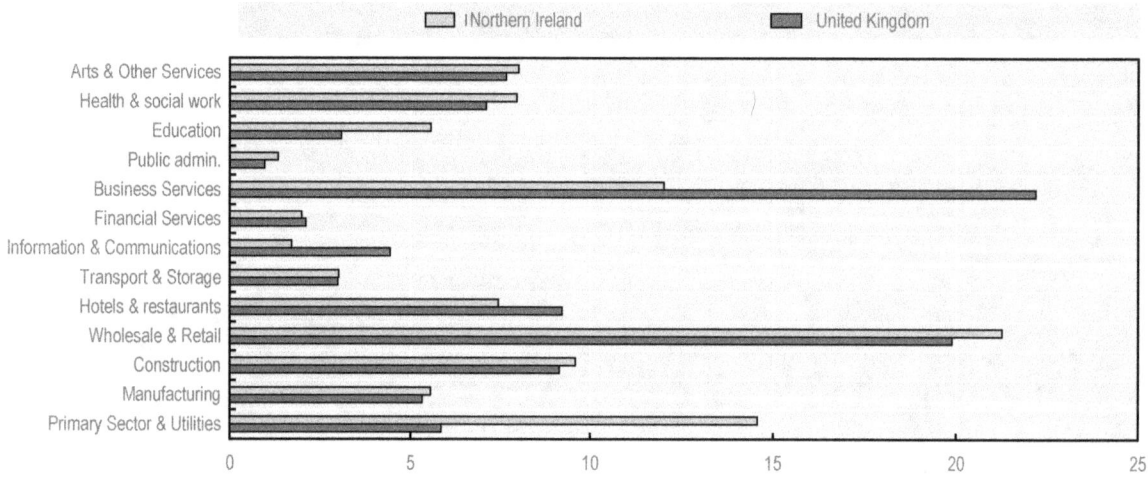

Source: UK Employer Skills Survey 2017.

StatLink https://doi.org/10.1787/888933903346

Figure 2.2 shows that the market in Northern Ireland is mainly local or national in comparison to the other countries of the United Kingdom. Nearly half of the enterprises in Northern Ireland sell their good or products locally, compared to 44% in Scotland and 43% in England, and less than 10% of exports internationally. While the share of goods and services sold to other countries in the European Union (EU) is similar to the rest of the UK, the international market outside the EU is very limited for Northern Ireland at less than 2%.

Figure 2.2. Geographical area in which the establishment's goods/services are primarily sold/serviced to the population, UK countries, 2017

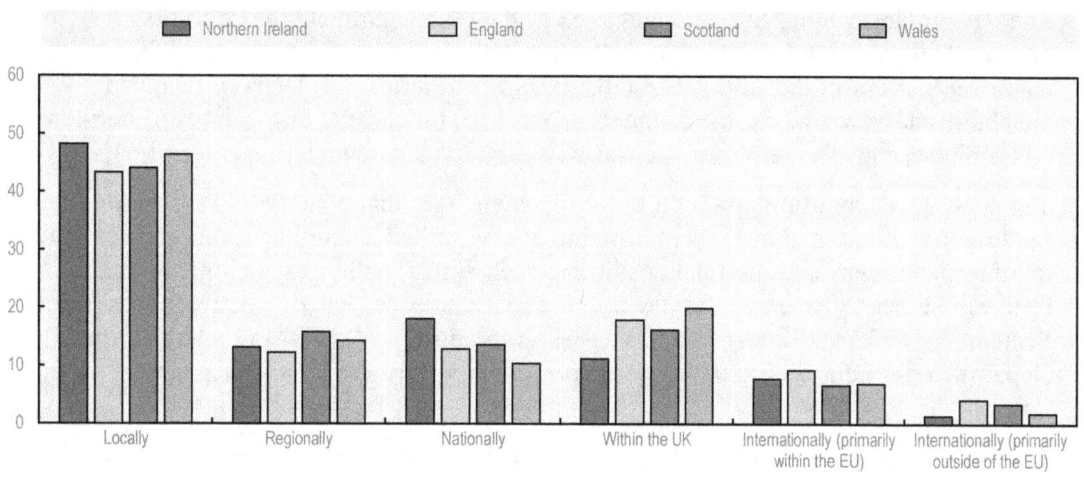

Source: UK Employer Skills Survey 2017.

StatLink https://doi.org/10.1787/888933903365

When looking at the classification of enterprises by funding/profit typology, in comparison to the other countries of the United Kingdom, Northern Ireland has the lowest share of profit-seeking establishments and the largest share of establishments operating in the charity/voluntary sector (Figure 2.3). This is reflected in the fact that GVA in Northern Ireland is generated to a large extent by the public administration, social services, education and human health sectors compared to the UK as a whole.

Figure 2.3. Share of enterprises by broad funding/profit typology, UK countries, 2017

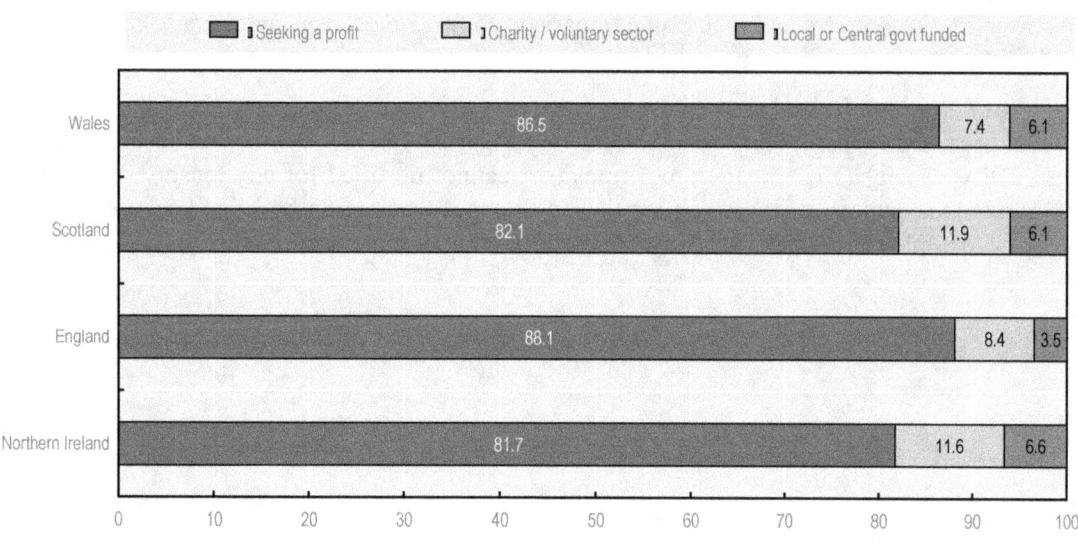

Source: UK Employer Skills Survey 2017.

StatLink https://doi.org/10.1787/888933903384

> **Box 2.1. The UK Employers Skills Survey**
>
> The UK Employer Skills Survey, conducted by the UK Department for Education, is based on over 87 000 telephone interviews with UK employers. Therefore, it is one of the largest employer surveys in the world. The most recent Northern Ireland survey involved 3 973 telephone interviews with establishments in Northern Ireland and 864 follow up interviews on training spend. The response rate was 64% slightly above the UK average of 62%.
>
> The survey gathers information on the skills challenges that employers face within their existing workforces and in terms of bringing in new skilled labour, the levels and nature of training investment and the relationship between skills challenges, training activity and business strategy. Research for the 2017 survey was carried out between April and September 2017 by IFF research, BMG research and Ipsos MORI on behalf of the UK Department for Education and their partners including Northern Ireland Department for the Economy.
>
> The survey findings are analysed by parliamentary constituency in Northern Ireland, but not at District Council level which is increasingly where the sub-regional focus lies. Given Northern Ireland's small size and that the fact that labour market policy is a regional issue, most research around employer needs tends to be more regionally focused.
>
> Initially the Employer Skills Survey was conducted by the UK Commission for Employment and Skills (UKCES) but, after its closure in March 2017, responsibility for the data collection and analysis passed to the UK Department for Education.

The incidence and typology of vacancies

Since 2015 all countries in the United Kingdom have increased the number of openings and around 20% of employers participating in the Employers Skills Survey had at least one vacancy at the time of the fieldwork. The growth in the recruitment activity was particularly strong in Northern Ireland where in comparison to 2015 there was an increase of 18% in the number of vacancies reported.

In 2017 Northern Ireland showed the lowest shares of vacancies in comparison to the other countries of the United Kingdom. As shown in Figure 2.4 below, this is true for both Hard to Fill vacancies (HtF) meaning positions that cannot be filled for any reason and skills shortage vacancies (SSVs) which are those vacancies that cannot be filled because of the lack of people having the relevant skills, qualification or experience to take the job.

Figure 2.4. Vacancies by type, UK countries, 2017

Share of total vacancies

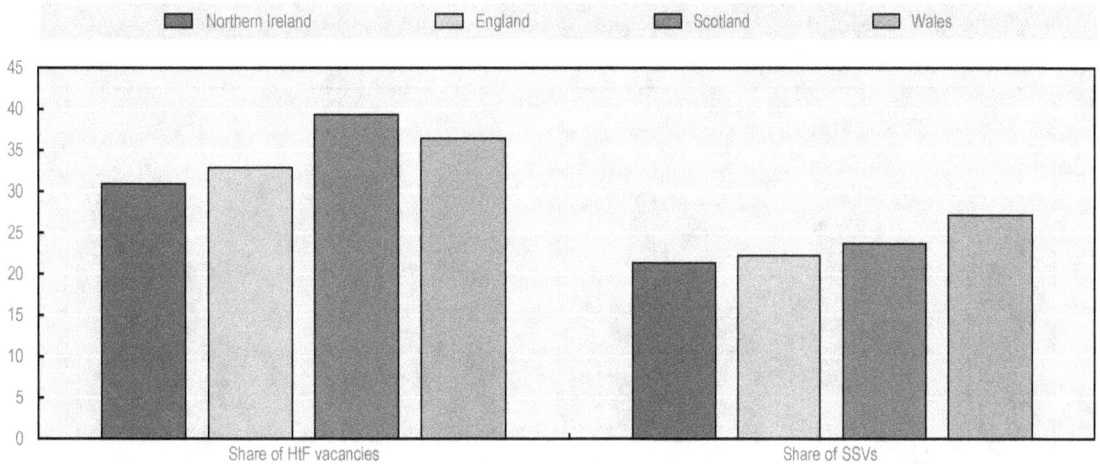

Note: Hard to Fill (HtF) vacancies refer to those positions that cannot be filled for any reason and skill shortage vacancies (SSV) refer to vacancies that cannot be filled because of the lack of people having the relevant skills, qualification or experience for the job.
Source: UK Employer Skills Survey 2017.

StatLink https://doi.org/10.1787/888933903403

While Northern Ireland has the lowest share of skills shortage vacancies compared to the other countries in the United Kingdom, the increase with the previous wave of the survey in 2015 was quite high (from 14% to 21% of total vacancies). In Northern Ireland, the regions with the highest share of skills shortage vacancies were the West (28%) and the East (27%).

It is also notable that since 2013 in England and Scotland the share of skills shortage vacancies has been stable while in Northern Ireland it decreased between 2011 and 2015 and went back to the 2011 levels in 2017. Irish enterprises affirmed that these vacancies increase the workload of their staff but also determine difficulties in meeting customer services objectives and in developing new product and services.

Figure 2.5. Skill shortage vacancies over time, UK countries, 2011-2017

Share of total number of vacancies

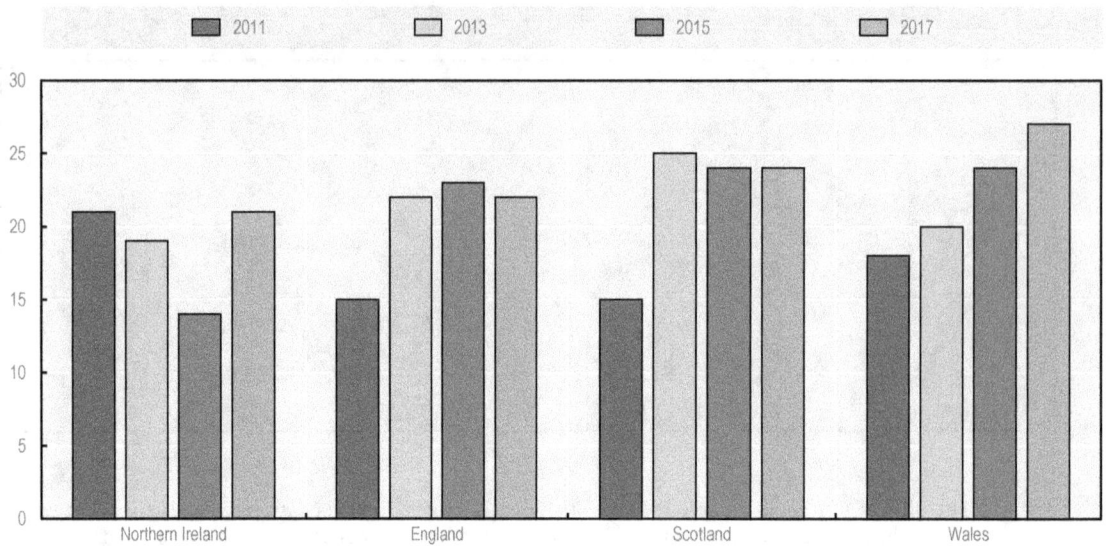

Source: UK Employer Skills Survey 2017.

StatLink https://doi.org/10.1787/888933903422

When looking at the incidence of vacancies by occupation, the distribution looks similar to the rest of the UK, with high values for associate professionals (high skills) and elementary occupations (low skills). The bigger difference is in medium skilled occupations and particularly for skilled trade occupations, where Northern Ireland has a higher incidence of vacancies and in caring, leisure and other services staff where values are higher for the UK (Figure 2.6).

Figure 2.6. Incidence of vacancies by occupation, United Kingdom and Northern Ireland, 2017

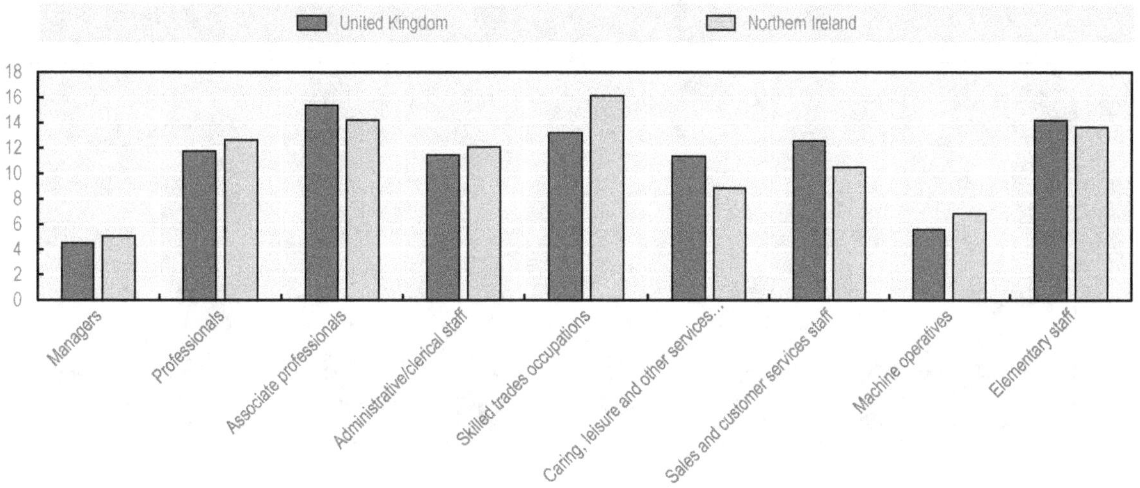

Source: UK Employer Skills Survey 2017.

StatLink https://doi.org/10.1787/888933903441

Training provision

Skills gaps also exist in the existing workforce mainly in the hotel and restaurant as well as the wholesale and retail sectors. In Northern Ireland, as highlighted above, also the current workforce has skills gaps mainly in skilled trade occupations.

To respond to these skills needs, training is broadly used in Northern Ireland to upskill the current workforce and increase their productivity. In 2017, 63% of employers offered training to their staff and 60% received a training in the last 12 months. This is a slight decrease from 2015 but the same trends can be observed for the other countries in the UK.

In all countries, a mix of on the job and off the job trainings are offered to the staff. In Northern Ireland similar to the Wales, these two types of training are offered equally to the workforce, while in England and Scotland on the job training seems to be more commonly used. Among employers offering training, 47% would like to train more while only 29% of employers who do not offer training would like to introduce it in their firms.

Similar to the UK average, in Northern Ireland, the two main raisons for upskilling are new legislative or regulatory requirements and the introduction of new technologies (both at 39%). However, the share of employers indicating the UK's decision to leave the European Union as an important factor is much higher than in the other countries of the UK except Scotland.

Figure 2.7. Type of training provided, UK countries, 2017

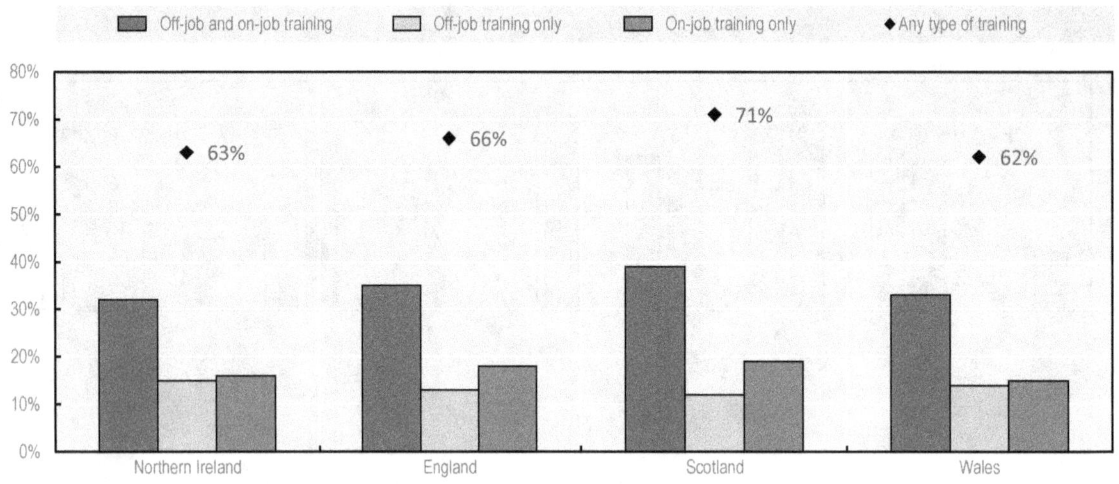

[Bar chart showing percentages for Northern Ireland, England, Scotland, and Wales across four training categories: Off-job and on-job training, Off-job training only, On-job training only, and Any type of training.

- Northern Ireland: Off-job and on-job ~32%, Off-job only ~15%, On-job only ~16%, Any type 63%
- England: Off-job and on-job ~35%, Off-job only ~13%, On-job only ~18%, Any type 66%
- Scotland: Off-job and on-job ~39%, Off-job only ~12%, On-job only ~19%, Any type 71%
- Wales: Off-job and on-job ~33%, Off-job only ~14%, On-job only ~15%, Any type 62%]

Source: UK Employer Skills Survey 2017

StatLink https://doi.org/10.1787/888933903460

Results from the OECD Survey of Northern Ireland firms

The right and successful implementation of apprenticeship schemes relies on local level implementation. This is why employers should play a significant role in shaping the demand for training courses and in contributing to skills development of the workforce. In order to capture their views in relation to their needs and to the benefits and issues they have in relation to the current apprenticeship scheme, a survey was sent from the Northern Ireland Chamber of Commerce to its members in May/ June 2017. The analysis presented in this chapter is based on 127 valid responses which provide general insights on these issues.

Business demography

Around half of the respondents to the survey can be classified as a small firms (i.e. having less than 49 employees), with slightly less than a quarter having less than 10 employees (micro enterprises). Considering that in Northern Ireland more than 95% of the firms have less than 49 employees, the distribution of responses by firm size highlights that bigger firms were more likely than smaller firms to respond to the survey. This is often the case as bigger firms have more human resources as well as more experience to answer.

Figure 2.8. Firm distribution by employment size, Northern Ireland

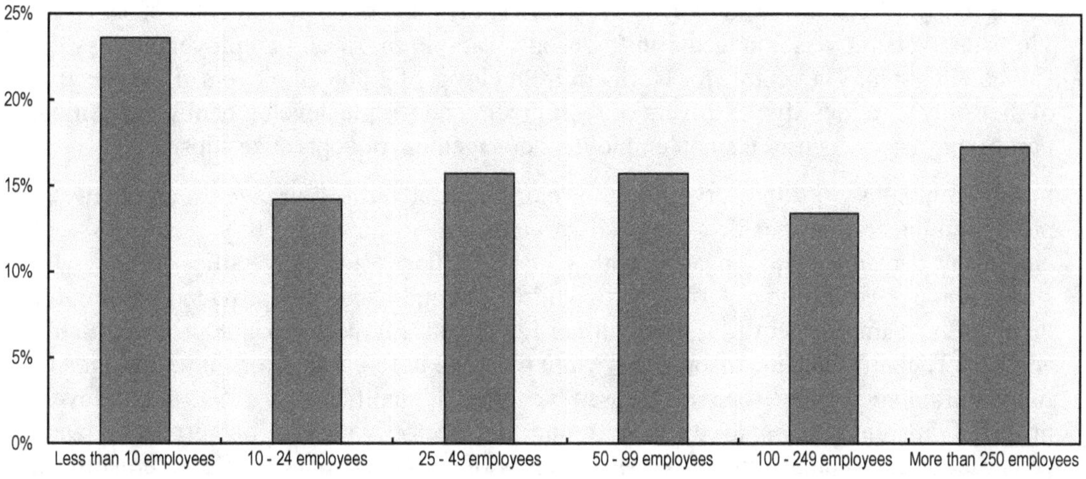

Source: OECD employers survey 2017

StatLink https://doi.org/10.1787/888933903479

When looking at the size of the workforce, in half of the firms in the sample the number of employees has increased in the past 12 months and it has decreased only in one in ten firms. In line with results in the first chapter of the report, this information confirms that the economic prospects of the region have improved in recent years.

The vast majority of surveyed firms operate in the services sector and less than 20% either in manufacturing or in construction. In terms of the area where the products are sold, slightly less than half of them are more oriented towards the international market and the rest mainly in Northern Ireland or rest of the United Kingdom. Only less than 10% operates in their local area.

Apprenticeships and skills

Apprenticeships schemes contribute to the improvement of the skills of the workforce and represent an effective pathway for young people in the school to work transition. As local employers play a significant role in determining the success of apprenticeships, the survey explores what are the skills needed across firms in Northern Ireland and what are the reasons for offering or not these types of schemes.

When looking at the skills that employers need to improve the productivity of their employees, 60% of firms indicated the need of technical skills specific to the job. As broadly recognised in the literature (OECD, 2015[19]) (OECD, 2016[20]), strong technical skills help businesses to become more productive and employees to gain marketable skills and feel more engaged in the company. In addition, organisational and planning skills as well as management skills are perceived as a need by employers of Northern Ireland. This type of skills can have an impact on the prevalence of High Performance Workplace Practices, which are often associated with better skills use at work (OECD/ILO, 2017[21]). Numeracy, literacy and IT skills, as well as foreign languages, do not seem to be a priority for employers.

> **Box 2.2. The Employer Perspective Survey**
>
> The Employer Perspectives Survey is a biennial study that has been conducted since 2010. The latest version was conducted in 2016 on a sample of 18 000 employers across the United Kingdom. The sample for Northern Ireland was of 2 000 employers. The objective of the study is to identify the drivers of recruitment and people development within firms. Part of the survey focuses also on employers' engagement in apprenticeships.
>
> In the 12 months prior the survey 44% of employers advertised vacancies, especially in public administration, health and social services and in the hospitality sectors.13% of employers declared being engaged with schools, colleges and universities to talk with students about career choices. Around two thirds of employers have provided training for their staff and among them 14% used Further Education (FE) colleges as source of training and 11% Higher Education institutions. More than one in five employers have arranged or funded training leading to a recognised vocational qualification. 13% of employers provided apprenticeships to their staff and the sector with the highest offer were construction and manufacturing. Nearly a quarter of employers plan to offer internships in the future.

As stated by a number of employers, the Levy scheme has increased the typologies of training providers that now can be other than colleges. This element of the new programme, will probably contribute to improve the offer of apprenticeships also for more qualified staff, including managers, and to respond to sector specific needs. In addition, employers express the need for training providers to have a better understanding of the industry in order to tailor an appropriate training programme on the basis of day-to-day operational work.

Figure 2.9. Skills needed to improve the productivity of employees, Northern Ireland

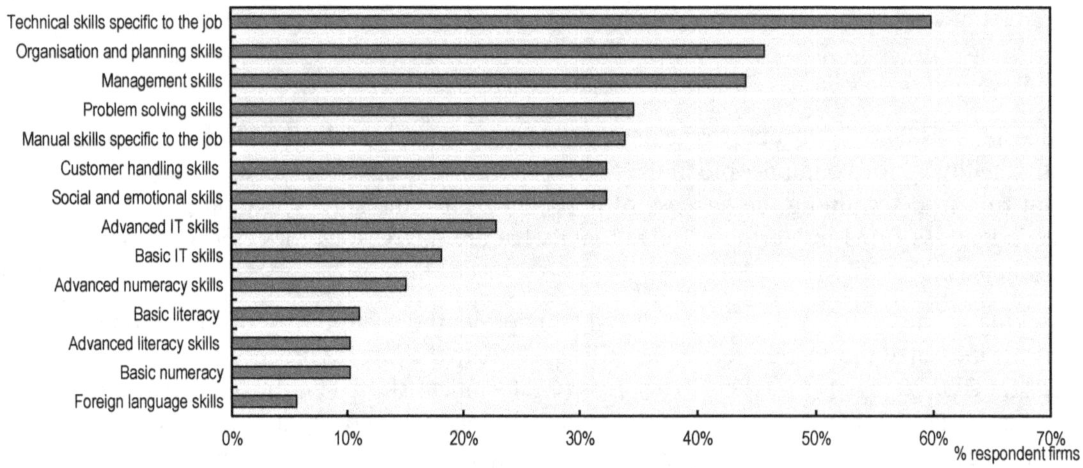

Source: OECD employers survey 2017

StatLink https://doi.org/10.1787/888933903498

Among respondents, less than half of the firms (44%) offered apprenticeships in the last 12 months. The main reasons for not offering an apprenticeship schemes were the lack of capacity (31%) and the lack of interest (21%) or need (20%). This result is probably related to the fact that the sample of the survey is mainly composed of SMEs which very often lack the human resources function required to undertake some of the administrative work necessary to participate in apprenticeship programmes. In addition, more awareness is required to inform employers about the benefits of apprenticeship or they do not or may have views that may not align with the current reality of the actual programme, which can often be customised and catered to their needs.

Figure 2.10. Reasons for not offering apprenticeships, Northern Ireland

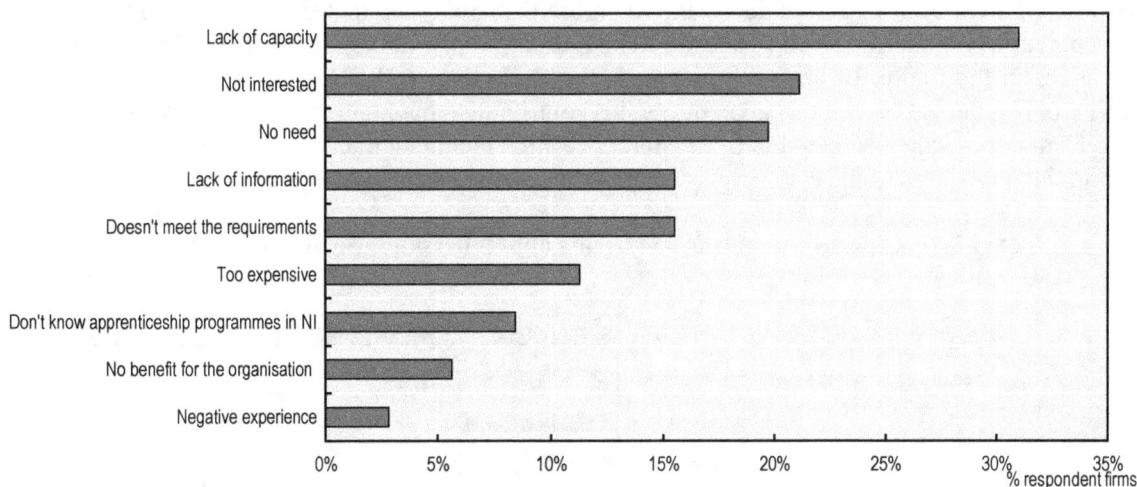

Note: Information is based on 71 responses corresponding to firms not offering apprenticeships
Source: OECD employers survey 2017

StatLink https://doi.org/10.1787/888933903517

Employers would like to have more support and engagement by both colleges and government bodies in promoting apprenticeships. First of all, schools and colleges should promote apprenticeship as a clear and valuable career option for young people. In particular, they should offer careers advice for young people who decide not to go to university. Families should be also involved in this process and helped to understand that vocational qualifications do not represent a "second class" route. Businesses across Northern Ireland seem willing to have apprentices and train part-time students. The experience of a number of firms who responded to the survey highlighted the fact that apprenticeships are often a better choice for those students who are clear about their career choice and benefit greatly from the opportunity to gain workplace experience whilst studying, often achieving professional qualifications much quicker than they would do if they had pursued a university degree course full time (OECD/ILO, 2017[22]).

Many employers stated that the government could have a more proactive role in promoting the benefits of apprenticeships as well as strengthening communication and collaboration with various trade bodies and business in order to have a better understanding of their current and future needs. Respondents also suggested that the government could identify a well-known business person or "public champion" who would help increasing awareness in relation to apprenticeships.

Secondly, businesses feel that secondary schools only have a limited understanding of their needs and the overall skills demand. In some local areas, efforts have been made to strengthen the relationships between schools and firms in different industrial sectors in order to improve the selection of candidates in relation to business needs. Thirdly, schools should make sure that entrants in apprenticeship schemes have good level of literacy, numeracy and IT skills after leaving compulsory education. Employers feel that if apprentices lack of basic skills, a big part of their apprenticeship focuses on that instead of offering the actual job training, learning the technical skills of the job.

Firms offering apprenticeships

The vast majority of firms have subsequently hired their apprentices, confirming that apprenticeship schemes are a good pathway to ease the entrance of young people into the labour market. More precisely 41% of the firms kept all of their apprentices while 38% kept more than two thirds of them. Among respondents, slightly more than 36% said that they would like to have more apprentices in the future and 16% the same amount. Only 12% said that they did not want apprentices in the future. In line with previous OECD findings (OECD/ILO, 2017[22]), the vast majority of respondents stated that apprenticeships contribute to maintain and improve skills levels of the firm. Other expected benefits from apprenticeships include attracting and retaining people and bringing new ideas to the company.

Figure 2.11. Expected benefits from offering apprenticeships, Northern Ireland

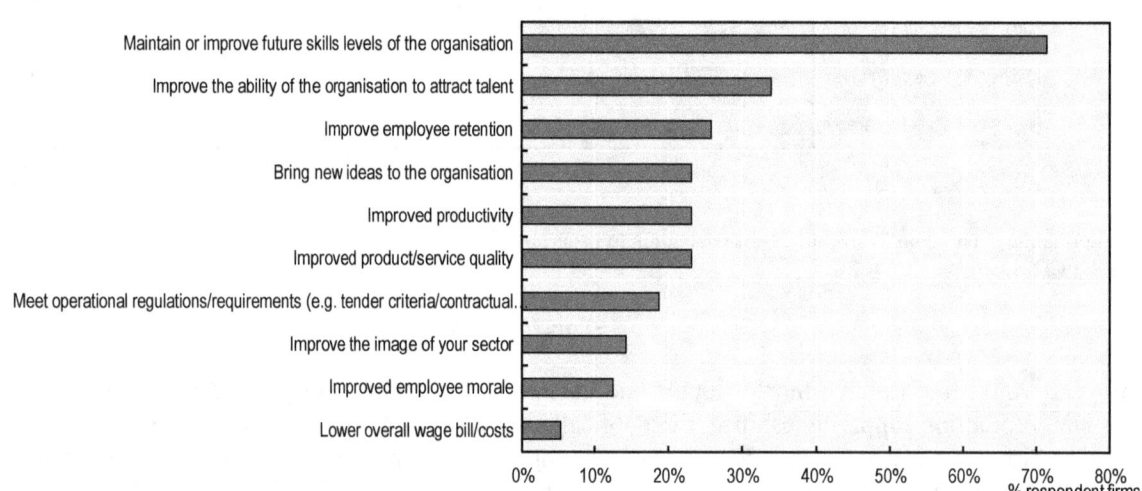

Note: Information is based on 112 responses corresponding to firms willing to offer apprenticeships in the future
Source: OECD employers survey 2017.

StatLink https://doi.org/10.1787/888933903536

Among firms offering apprenticeships schemes, only 16% had unfilled apprenticeships positions over the last 12 months, meaning that generally these types of schemes have a relatively high take up rate. However, employers also admit having some concerns about apprenticeships programmes currently in place; nearly a third affirm being worried about high drop out during apprenticeship and just under a quarter worried about not having enough applicants.

Figure 2.12. Concerns about apprenticeship programmes currently in place, Northern Ireland

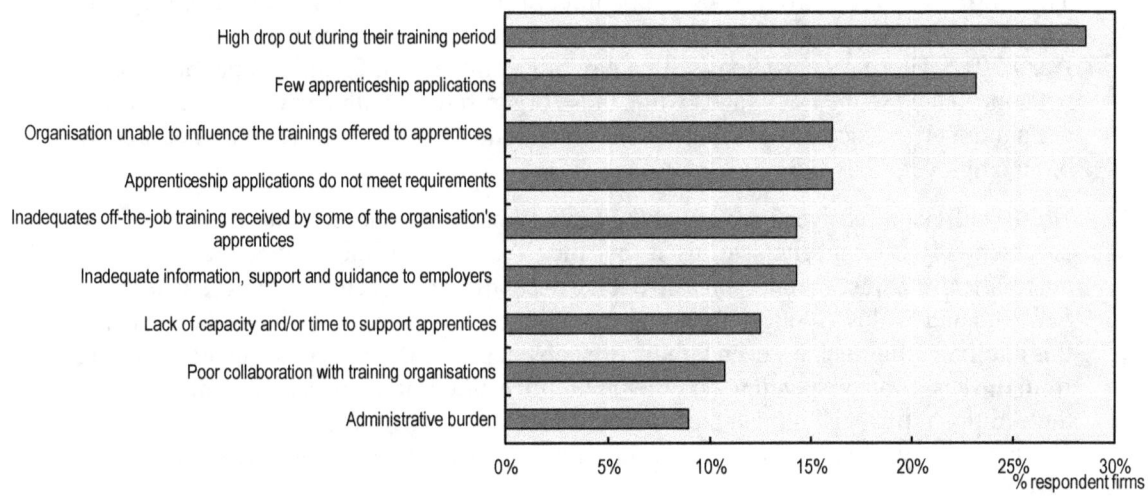

Note: Information is based on 56 responses corresponding to firms having offered apprenticeships in the past
Source: OECD employers survey 2017.

StatLink https://doi.org/10.1787/888933903555

Employer reaction to the Apprenticeship Levy scheme

While a high number of employers consider apprenticeships very useful for their growth, some concerns exist in relation to the implementation of the Apprenticeship Levy scheme, which was introduced across the UK in 2017 (see box).

> **Box 2.3. The Apprenticeship Levy**
>
> The introduction of a UK wide Apprenticeship Levy was first announced by the Chancellor in the summer 2015 Budget Statement and was subsequently introduced in April 2017. Those organisations with a pay bill of more than £3 million per annum are net contributors to the Levy funds while those organisations with a pay bill of £3 million per annum or less do not contribute to the Levy funds. The Levy is set at a rate of 0.5% of an employer's pay bill.
>
> Northern Ireland receives its share of the Levy through the Barnett consequential which is essentially the mechanism used by the Treasury in the United Kingdom to automatically adjust the amounts of public expenditure allocated to Northern Ireland, Scotland and Wales to reflect changes in spending levels. However, in Northern Ireland this additional funding has been largely offset by negative Barnett consequentials arising from the cessation of spending on other apprenticeship programmes and combined with the additional financial burden the Levy will place on public sector employers, means in reality the Levy will not result in any noticeable additional funding being made available.
>
> The levy has therefore come across as essentially a tax on business. It has been viewed as complicated, of very little benefit, and it probably has potential costs. Skills policy, including responsibility for apprenticeships, is a fully devolved matter, so each administration across the UK has developed an apprenticeship policy tailored to meet the needs of their own skills priorities. Notwithstanding the introduction of the Levy, each administration will continue to set their own policies and priorities in relation to skills and apprenticeships.

Employers reported that there are too many governing bodies and agencies are involved in the scheme and there is a lack of strategy and coordination among them. This slows down its implementation and reduces the effective use of funds that should be devoted to apprenticeships. At the time of the OECD survey, a number of employers seem to be not aware of the different programmes offered in Northern Ireland. In particular, they would like to have more support and guidance on how to fully benefit from the apprenticeship levy scheme. Employers reported that they require more clarity in relation to the wages and the eligibility criteria of the new scheme.

SMEs reported concern about the current apprentice system as it is too complicated for small organisations that often do not possess a dedicated human resources function and may lack capacity in applying for government supports available for employing apprentices. In addition, SMEs reported difficulties with regard to the organisation of the in-school portion of the apprenticeship training. As most apprenticeship courses commence in September, recruitment of apprentices must be completed by August but often the needs of small firms rise during the year and without a very precise planning but for them is not possible to take apprentices.

A number of employers also find the new scheme should be more flexible. In particular, they consider the age limit (i.e. 25 years old), the access to the levy fund as well as the training provision to a number of sectors is too restrictive for the Northern Irish labour market. In addition, the fact that employment in the public sector is high in Northern Ireland makes the implementation of the scheme harder in Northern Ireland than in the rest of the United Kingdom. Some employers suggested the implementation of a public sector apprenticeship programme where government agencies can bid into to support recruitment of public sector apprentices.

Conclusions

Employers participating in the OECD survey report some positive experiences of having apprentices within their workforce. One of the main reasons for not offering apprenticeship training relates to the lack of human resources and administrative capacities. This is not an unsurprising result given the high share of SMEs operating within the Northern Irish economy, which generally do not have a human resources function. Employers in Northern Ireland are concerned by the high dropout rate of participants in apprenticeship schemes; therefore, more should be done to increase effectiveness of apprenticeship programmes by ensuring the delivery of learning is flexible, for example by offering part-time training or modular courses. Finally, employers would like to have more support from the government and further explanations regarding the levy scheme and how to fully benefit from it.

References

Department for Education (2018), *Employer skills survey 2017*, https://assets.publishing.service.gov.uk/government/uploads/system/uploads/attachment_data/file/746493/ESS_2017_UK_Report_Controlled_v06.00.pdf (accessed on 26 October 2018). [1]

Northern Ireland Assembly (2016), *The Executive's Forthcoming Revised Economic Strategy for Northern Ireland: Preliminary Considerations*, http://www.niassembly.gov.uk/globalassets/documents/raise/publications/2016-2021/2016/economy/8116.pdf (accessed on 26 October 2018). [2]

OECD (2016), "Skills for a Digital World: 2016 Ministerial Meeting on the Digital Economy Background Report", *OECD Digital Economy Papers*, No. 250, OECD Publishing, Paris, http://dx.doi.org/10.1787/5jlwz83z3wnw-en. [4]

OECD (2015), *OECD Science, Technology and Industry Scoreboard 2015: Innovation for growth and society*, OECD Publishing, Paris, http://dx.doi.org/10.1787/sti_scoreboard-2015-en. [3]

OECD/ILO (2017), *Better Use of Skills in the Workplace: Why It Matters for Productivity and Local Jobs*, OECD Publishing, Paris, http://dx.doi.org/10.1787/9789264281394-en. [5]

OECD/ILO (2017), *Engaging Employers in Apprenticeship Opportunities: Making It Happen Locally*, OECD Publishing, Paris, http://dx.doi.org/10.1787/9789264266681-en. [6]

Chapter 3. Implementing employer engagement strategies in Northern Ireland

This chapter highlights examples of programmes in Northern Ireland that aim to engage employers in vocational education and training delivery. It also highlights recent initiatives to develop a national strategy for career guidance as well as better anticipate the future skills needs of the Northern Irish economy. It also provide an overview of recent actions by District Councils to implement local employment and skills strategies.

Understanding how employers are engaging with government on skills needs

Formal governance bodies to engage and consult employers on skills

In Northern Ireland, the skill needs of employers are voiced through different representative bodies including the NI Chamber of Commerce, Confederation of British Industry (CBI), Invest NI and Federation of Small Business (FSB). Matrix is the Northern Ireland Science Industry Panel, a business led expert industry panel formed to advise government, industry and academia on the commercial exploitation of R&D and science and technology in Northern Ireland and whose role includes help to the business community to inform government policy. This includes advice on priority sectors and priority skills for business.

Sector Skills Councils (SSCs) and Sector Training Councils (STCs) also provide a platform for employers to express their demands for skills training. The Sector Skills Councils provide sector specific advice on skills development for employees doing particular jobs. They are independent employer led organisations that provide a range of services to help employers to reduce skills shortages and improve learning standards. Each Sector Skills Councils will agree on priorities and with its employers and partners to reducing skills gaps and shortages; improving productivity, business and performance; increase opportunities to boost the skills and productivity of everyone in the sector's workforce, including action on equal opportunities; and improving learning supply to include apprenticeships, higher education and national occupational standards.

Box 3.1. Sector Training Councils in Northern Ireland

Sector Training Councils were established in 1994 as independent employer representative bodies in Northern Ireland. There are currently eight in operation in Northern Ireland. They include the Construction Industry Training Board (CITB), Electrical Training Trust (ETT), Engineering Training Council, Food & Drink Sector Skills, Northern Ireland Screen, NI Polymers Association and Transport Training Services. Their role is to articulate the skills, education and training needs of their sectors in the short and long term; advise on training standards required for their sectors; and work with the Department for the Economy (DfE) and SSCs to ensure that training needs and standards are met.

It has been challenging keeping SSCs and STCs involved and operational. Many of their funding structures have changed from being central government funded to become self-funded and only some of these organisations have survived. Some still exist in Northern Ireland and some are based only in England. For example, the Food & Drink Sector Skills in Northern Ireland is now self-funded through its own reserves and through support projects including an education programme in schools. The Electrical Training Trust, for example, provides advice and support services to employers in the electrical contracting sector with apprentice recruitment and skills training needs.

This includes liaison with the careers service, post primary schools and other support agencies on behalf of local industry. However, constraints and shifts in local government policy brought about an end to the organisations lengthy history in training apprentice electricians. Until 2016, the organisation had successfully recruited and trained over 5 000 apprentice electricians in the local economy.

One of the most recent initiatives has been Tech Partnership (formerly "e-skills UK") which is the UK's sector skills council for the IT industry representing the interests of employers to ensure that the UK is equipped to manage the worldwide digital marketplace. While the organisation closed in 2018, many of its activities are now carried out by other institutions and government departments. These organisations had a crucial role to play in the 'Success through STEM' Strategy from the Department for Education and the then Department for Employment and Learning which placed a strong emphasis on business (in terms of private sector employers) in growing the supply of STEM skills into the local workforce (Department of education,(n.d.)[23]). Employers were viewed to have the key role to play in improving the attractiveness of the STEM sector and in highlighting the opportunities that exist locally and in working with the supply side to articulate demand and ensure that the courses that are in place meet their needs.

> **Box 3.2. STEM champions in Northern Ireland: Gearing to the skills system to emerging and innovative sectors**
>
> A Business sub group, chaired by a STEM Champion was established to lead a network of stakeholders, including the relevant Sector Skills Councils, STEM charity bodies, Business Education Partnerships (BEPs) and other employer representative bodies to work with local companies and facilitate their engagement with both students and teachers within local schools, further education colleges and universities to promote STEM. However when the Department for Enterprise, Trade and Investment and the Department for Education and Learning were merged in 2016/17, the STEM Business Group was put on hold while the strategy was reviewed and has not been reconstituted since then. The role of STEM Champion is no longer an official departmental position but the original STEM champion maintains contact with the department on all things STEM and has taken over the responsibility for the production of the STEM Supplement through Catalyst Inc. Twice a year, Catalyst Inc and Matrix, the Northern Ireland Science Panel, work with industry, government and education to publish a STEM Courses and Careers Supplement which is aimed to provide information to pupils, teachers and parents about the career opportunities and pathways.

Finally, the Collaborative Networks programme is a more sectorally focused initiative in Northern Ireland. Through this network programme, Invest NI supports business-led collaborative networks to stimulate economic development within Northern Ireland (Invest NI, 2015[24]). The objective of the support is to develop the capability and capacity of regional clusters/networks by attracting private sector companies, investors, researchers and academia to maximise collaborative opportunities in the development of new products, processed or services.

Invest NI engaged with sectors to identify common skills needs and helped facilitate a response from training providers. For example, companies have had particularly issues with a lack of software engineers. Invest NI worked with the universities to increase the number of places and part-time masters in computer science as well as with companies to increase their upskilling investment levels in this field. A collaborative approach between employers and Invest NI in addressing skills needs can be also found in advanced engineering, agri-food, hospitality and tourism sectors.

Invest NI also facilitated effective employer engagement in developing the Software and Systems Design A Level. Invest NI has acted as broker for industry in designing the A level. They have been doing this on an on-going basis ultimately to ensure a better connection and alignment of business needs.

Better gearing the skills system to the labour market

National strategy for career guidance

The government also provides a publicly funded Careers Service that is delivered by 95 professionally qualified Careers Advisors in 27 locations including Careers Resource Centres, Job Centres and Jobs & Benefits offices throughout Northern Ireland (OECD, 2014[10]). There is a well-defined strategy for careers guidance in Northern Ireland called *'Preparing for Success'* which sets out the Executive's aim to support people to make the best decisions for their careers (Department for the Economy,(n.d.)[25]). The initiative is a joint strategy between the Department of Education and the Department for the Economy. The Strategy aims to ensure that young people and adults will:

- have access to good quality careers education provision, up-to-date labour market information, and impartial careers information, advice and guidance, to assist them to make well-informed career choices, to achieve their potential and prosper in employment;
- be lifelong learners and be motivated to pursue continuous professional development to achieve their own potential, to become effective employees and to make a valuable contribution to the local economy;
- develop the skills to plan their career, and manage planned and unplanned career change; and
- have a clear understanding of the impact of their education, training and employment choices and make career choices which are informed and well thought through and based on self-awareness; understand the relevance of their education, skills and experience; and be aware of the opportunities and pathways available.

This includes more and better work experience for young people and improved access to impartial advice. A key feature of the Strategy is to ensure that the careers system going forward will be able to secure a balance between the needs of the individual, employers and the wider economy within the guidance process. It aims to ensure that all career advisors continue to have a number of placements with employers in growth sectors each year.

Through the Careers Advisory Forum (CAF), the government develops strategic and local partnerships to better understand the employability skills, qualifications and attributes needed by employers to grow their business (Department for the Economy,(n.d.)[26]). With the support of the CAF, there is an emphasis on facilitating better links between schools, colleges, local businesses, local councils and enterprise agencies. Employers are engaged to attract more people, and in particular young people, to consider careers in priority, growth and emerging sectors (see Box 3.3). The government also encourages employer participation by providing support and guidance to employers in the delivery of work experiences; and exploring how teachers can access relevant work placements to help them better understand current and future local labour market opportunities.

> **Box 3.3. Careers Advisory Forum in Northern Ireland**
>
> The role of the Careers Advisory Forum is to advise the government on current and future Careers provision in the context of the refreshed Careers Strategy 2015-2020; facilitate system level engagement between employers, educators and other key stakeholders, including parents, to support them in their advisory role; and support local level stakeholder involvement with service users and the education and business sectors. There is strong representation of the business and the education sectors, including business bodies, youth entrepreneurship, Education Authority, Parenting NI, Colleges NI, Education & Training Inspectorate (ETI), CCEA and others. They have working groups focusing on three strands of work: i) School-employer engagement; ii) Work experience; and iii) Upskilling the existing workforce.
>
> The first strand of the work includes greater encouragement/support of teachers/lecturers and trainers on how to spend time with employers to better understand their needs, develop a best practice model for local engagement between Area Learning Communities (voluntary coalitions of schools in different areas to support collaborative working and greater access to occupational studies) and employers, increase employer representation on local school and college Board of Governors, encouraging employers to articulate skills needs through established Government digital portals (e.g. ccea.org.uk) and encourage employers to support teachers, lecturers and trainers through Continuous Professional Development (CPD) activities that improves understanding of the modern work place.
>
> The second strand includes encouragement of more employers to provide work experience through Connect to Success (see below) and ensure that all pupils have good quality work-related learning experiences including work placements. The last strand focuses on the role of the Careers Service and others in better engagement with employers on upskilling and reskilling including ways of showcasing best practice examples of how Northern Ireland employers, particularly SMEs, have successfully upskilled their workforce. There is a dedicated careers website hosted by NIDirect that points individuals to the various paths to interact with Careers Advisors including online chat, email, phone and at the 25 offices located across Northern Ireland. It also provides access to different online career tools for both young people and adults. The Department for the Economy is currently procuring additional software so that up front labour market information is available further explore trend data.

Northern Ireland has had the advantage of significant Ministerial buy in for careers approaches. There has been good collaboration at the Executive level across all political parties. The system is viewed as agile and flexible with a short chain between the Minister and delivery on the ground. In England, schools have a statutory responsibility to provide careers advice but have no ring-fenced budget. Scotland and Wales have arms-length bodies doing careers (private and public funding). For example, Skills Development Scotland is the national skills body supporting the people and businesses of Scotland to develop and apply their skills.

In Northern Ireland the role of careers advisor in schools is being diminished by falling budgets. Teachers and not careers professionals are typically responsible for the careers advisor role. There is still a belief in Northern Ireland that the higher education system is the pinnacle of achievement and a significant job is needed to convince parents and teachers particularly but also students that apprenticeships/high level apprenticeships are of significant value in developing a strong career.

The objective of the Apprenticeship NI 2017 strategy is to ensure that apprenticeships are held in equally high esteem to higher education and to provide a direct route into a range of occupations and sectors previously only accessible through traditional higher education pathways. There have been definite inroads made into highlighting the advantages of pursuing apprenticeships and other forms of vocational training as a career. It will take further investment of time and effort to convince all parents in Northern Ireland that this is a strong and viable career option.

The implementation of career guidance programmes in Northern Ireland

Careers guidance is a compulsory part of the curriculum in Northern Ireland and each school must provide support to its students on this matter. However, the Executive is not prescriptive about what schools have to teach rather it specifies a minimum content and schools have autonomy on the delivery. There is no separate funding available for this and it must be met out of each school's budget. Each school is inspected on its careers education content on career's education although largely focusing on 'best practice' guidance. This flexibility about the way career guidance is implemented means that it varies significantly across schools in the country on the basis of funds and school's priority. For example, some schools teach careers from Year 8 while others do not teach careers until Year 10.

Careers guidance comes under the subject of Learning for Life and Work (LLW) which is a core part of the curriculum from Key Stage (KS) 3 and 4 aimed at helping young people develop the fundamental skills, knowledge, qualities and dispositions that are pre-requisites for life and work. At KS4, LLW includes the contributory elements of employability, local and global citizenship and personal development. The main focus however is to try to give students skills to make the right choices and recognise that there is no 'job for life'. It is therefore about self-awareness, skills and aptitudes, that is, how to look at the labour market and match up with jobs/skills in labour market. There is a section on entrepreneurship, and then a specific section on career management which schools are required to teach. LLW is a GCSE but also part of the wider curriculum. The Department for Education also expects careers guidance to be built into all subjects taught at school. This is so that students can see the relevance of each subject to careers recognising that curriculum and careers need to go together and be economically relevant.

There are 95 professionally qualified Careers Advisers employed by the Department for the Economy in Northern Ireland. In 2016/2017, 201 post-primary schools (66 grammar and 135 secondary) and 39 dedicated special schools have partnership agreements. These agreements are in place will all statutory funded post primary schools in NI which define the careers support which will be delivered to students at key points in careers decision making. In the past some schools were reluctant to avail of this offer, but in recent years participation has increased. The Careers strategy contains a commitment to provide face to face impartial advice to at least 95% of all the year 12 cohort. In addition, all year 10 pupils received help from the Careers Service when making choices for GCSE. The aim of this partnership approach is to compliment the careers education programme with personalised careers guidance to widen and deepen a young person's understanding of the world of work.

An inquiry into Careers education and advice in Northern Ireland set out evidence from the Northern Ireland Schools and Colleges Careers Association that the careers advice offered in schools and colleges is of variable standard due to a lack of or old qualifications and lack of staff dedicated specifically to careers advice.

Better gearing the education system to the labour market

The Education and Training Inspectorate's Chief Executive's report (2014-2016) highlighted that 99% of post-primary schools provide well-informed, impartial careers education, information, advice and guidance alongside relevant, well-planned and challenging workplace experiences for the pupils (The Education and Training Inspectorate, 2016[27]). However, links with local employers seem to be underdeveloped and, more generally, insufficient attention is paid to the coherent development of the skills needed in the local economy.

In work-based learning, a majority of the provision is better structured: there is an appropriate focus on establishing successful career progression pathways for the trainees and apprentices who are mostly knowledgeable, well-informed and supported with up-to-date insightful information within their sectors. The curriculum provision for senior pupils has a highly effective focus on employability skills and innovative programmes of careers education, information, advice and guidance.

The most effective careers provision is characterised by well-informed, impartial careers education, information, advice and guidance and relevant, well-planned and challenging workplace experiences for pupils which enhance their employability and inform individual career planning. In the less effective practice, insufficient attention is paid to the coherent development of the skills and attitudes valued by employers, including resilience, resourcefulness, team-working and the ability to communicate effectively.

There is a commitment in the Programme for Government to look at school employer engagement (Education and Training Inspectorate, 2016[28]). Under Outcome 1 – *We prosper through a strong, competitive, regionally balanced economy* – there is a commitment to 'create an environment to promote and enable innovation' which includes a commitment to increase the integration of education and work – supporting schools to embed innovation, creativity and entrepreneurship at all levels of education from primary to career development and to strengthen the knowledge exchange system between universities, colleges and businesses.

In February 2017, the then Ministers for Education and the Economy agreed that the two Departments should work together to develop a more strategic, joined up approach to 14-19 education and training provision with a focus on the achievement of outcomes. The project aims to develop a joint DE/DfE strategy on education and training which should deliver appropriate flexible routes through education where young people aged 14-19 are fully informed about coherent and relevant possible pathways. The initiative supports the overarching aims of the draft Programme for Government, draft Industrial Strategy and the NICS Outcomes Delivery Plan 2018/19 which recognise the high value of education and skills in preparing young people for life and work.

The Departments have developed a draft vision statement for education for 14-19 year olds called 'Educating all our young people to help shape their future in a prosperous Northern Ireland'. This statement assumes that clear pathways through education would exist so that young people can progress to achieve their full potential. It should deliver clearly defined routes through education, making the best use of the resources available and enabling every young persons to make good careers decisions and to acquire the knowledge, skills and qualifications (general and/or professional and technical) to secure meaningful employment and contribute to society and the economy.

The Departments held an Innovation Lab in early August with a wide range of stakeholders participating to examine the key issues. The report from the event is being used to scope the activities necessary and the Departments have put in place a joint team to progress this complex area of work.

Training for Success is a programme designed for young people aged 16-17 (or under 22/24 years for those with extended eligibility entitlement) which provides training to give them the tools and skills they need to get a job. The training provides young people with relevant qualifications as well as the required personal and behavioural skills to progress into work. There are four options, each of which comprises a common curriculum of Essential Skills, personal and social development skills, employability skills, and professional and technical skills. One aspect of the programme is a work placement which allows young people the opportunity to develop their professional and technical skills and employability skills. For example, SERC which is one of Northern Ireland's regional colleges, has over 600 young people on TFS all of whom require work placements as part of their programme. The college currently works with over 500 employers across 22 disciplines to secure work placements. SERC employs a team of 16 Training Support Officers to help secure a work placement suitable to the young person's needs. They make contact with employers and assess all potential work placements around suitability for that young person to develop their skills along with any barriers that person may have and ensure standards are met in terms of accessibility and health and safety.

Collaboration with firms in gearing career guidance to demand

An objective of the *"Preparing for Success'* Strategy is to ensure that all career advisors continue to have a number of placements with employers in growth sectors each year (Department for the Economy,(n.d.)[25]). The Careers Advisors must have a least five exposures to the world of work which includes visits, industry placements and perhaps on-going relations with companies. The Food industry in Northern Ireland was one of first sectors to have careers people into their companies to see what they did and the jobs/skills on offer. This has been going on for 4 or 5 years.

The Careers Strategy is a joint Strategy between the Department of Education and Department for Economy reflecting the importance of making the link between teachers/trainees and industry. A Careers Strategy Steering Group (comprising senior officials from both departments) was established to oversee the implementation of the updated Careers Strategy. The Steering Group has developed two joint action plans for 2015/17 and 2016/17 which have been completed. A draft action plan for the 2018-2020 period has been developed but in the absence of Ministers has not been signed off. Officials are progressing some of the actions contained in the draft plan.

There have been no actions from a Northern Ireland Executive perspective in engaging teachers with industry until recently. It has been down to each school and this has meant that the approach has been quite ad hoc. This research would suggest that some schools are better than others. Some schools do send their teachers out into the business environment. An example is St Mary's High School in Downpatrick where the principal requires every teacher to have experience in industry.

This is becoming more strategic with the draft Programme for Government and Industrial Strategy. For example, there is a commitment in the draft Programme for Government to look at school employer engagement. The Department of Education has recently undertaken a survey of schools to ascertain a baseline position in relation to the types and extent of school employer engagement. The findings of this survey will help inform future work in this area

The local Councils are becoming increasingly involved through their Community Planning process. They can be a strong catalyst for bringing together schools and local employers. Armagh City, Banbridge and Craigavon are involved in this through a community-planning workshop involving the Department for the Economy also. Belfast City Council is also strong in this regard.

Online resources

There are a number of online careers tools currently accessible from the NIdirect website (https://www.nidirect.gov.uk/campaigns/careers). They include *'Career starter'* (11 to 13 year olds) to help students match their skills and interests with future career options and help them choose what subjects to study. The match is based on what people are interested in and what they are good at. There is an on-line tool called *'Career Ideas'* intended to be used by 14-19 year olds which suggests and helps students explore different career options. Further improvements and additional online tools are expected to be implemented by April 2019.

Connect to Success NI is an online central system launched in September 2017 that the Department for the Economy (DfE) have developed to advertise work experience opportunities for young people. The main objectives are to:

- provide employers with an online platform on which advertise their work experience opportunities.
- give employers access to a wide range of young people to promote their company and the skills they need for the future.
- broaden awareness of the range of occupations that exist across all sectors in Northern Ireland.

The online system aims to i) reduce burden on schools to find placements; ii) improve access for all and iii) for employers to show case what they have on offer. Since summer 2017 all apprenticeship opportunities are included on the Connect to Success portal.

It has been challenging getting employers on board. Time is the key issue even though the point of Connect to Success is to help cut down on the time taken for employers to secure work placements and apprenticeships. The Chair of the CAF has worked with business bodies and others to highlight business responsibility to advertising vacancies on the portal. Employers need to communicate better about what they need although there is a view that employers have to be educated about what they need.

NIbusinessinfo.co.uk contains detailed advice and links for employers to follow up on apprenticeship programmes. This is Northern Ireland based. There is also a link on higher education training opportunities for business but the link takes you to a UK Training Gateway. There is also a link to a Graduate Talent Pool which is also a UK wide initiative.

There is a dedicated website where employers can advertise apprenticeship positions. Connect to Success NI is an online central system that the Department for the Economy have developed to advertise work experience opportunities for young people. Connect to Success NI went 'live' in September 2016 and the hope is that the online system can benefit employers and young people in a range of ways.

Employers can also advertise vacancies on the Employers Online NI website which enables employers to notify and manage their job vacancies online from their desktops. It helps employers to fill vacancies and jobseekers to find employment through the display of full and accurate vacancy information. Employers can also contact their local Jobs and Benefits offices and Jobcentres websites as well as contact their local further education college, university or contracted training provider who may be aware of potential employees.

Regional colleges also extensively advertise apprenticeship and work-based training programmes. For example, Southern Regional College has *'The Job Hub'* where employers can advertise vacancies for apprenticeships and higher level apprenticeships.

Better anticipating future skills needs of Northern Ireland

In 2015, the Department for Education and Learning (DEL) launched the NI Skills Barometer which has been developed by the University of Ulster's Economic Policy Centre (UUEPC) (Department for the Economy,(n.d.)[29]). This is a detailed modelling exercise to estimate future skills needs and gaps by level, sector and subject area across the country. This includes analysis of:

- *Job growth* – including both expansion demand (when sectors grow or contract) and replacement demand (e.g. people leave due to retirement, for family reasons or to move to another sector and they must be replaced);
- *Changing skills mix* – based on previous trends and related to the increasing the level of skills in the workforce across all sectors; and
- *Supply of skills into the economy*.

After the first publication of the Skills Barometer research in November 2015, significant engagement has occurred across a wide range of stakeholders to complement the quantitative findings of the research. In particular, the following stakeholders were involved: careers advisors to help inform young people and their parents when choosing future career pathway; teachers and schools to contribute to curriculum development; business groups to develop and articulate skills needs; and Department for the Economy and wider Government to inform policy development and level of provision to meet skills needs of the NI economy.

A wide range of sectoral bodies, rather than individual employers were consulted to obtain their views on skills requirements across a number of sectors. These include People First representing the retail and hospitality sector, the Construction Industry Training Board (CITB) representing the construction sector, and Food & Drink Sector Skills representing the Agri-Food sector. A number of other sectoral bodies had been involved but are not longer in existence, for example, e-skills representing the IT sector. The sectoral bodies were consulted to further study employment projections for their sectors, the typical annual requirement of staff from education, the current and projected sectoral skills mix of the sector and the qualifications needed for each sector and occupation. The interaction with the sectoral bodies also involved discussions around emerging skills, skills that should be incorporated into existing qualifications and the most important subject areas for work in a particular sector.

As a consequence of the challenges faced by a number of Sector Skills Councils, the involvement of employers in the Skills Barometer has been relatively difficult. Those employers that have contributed to this initiative were part of sectors that recognise the importance of understanding and anticipating future skills need and that have enough funds to support employers participation in this exercise. Another issue faced when listening to sectoral bodies was that they invariably all needed more people with skills relevant to their sector.

The Skills Barometer is an important source of information about skills needs and employers are extensively consulted before its production. The Department for the Economy is also looking at new techniques to identify skills requirements using, for example, web scraping of job vacancy sites. The Department for the Economy is working with UUEPC to supplement the Skills Barometer with additional labour market information and present this in an interactive and user-friendly approach. It has been recognised that it is important that all can understand it and teachers and others have been asking for this. This will be part of the new online careers software that the Careers Service are currently developing.

Box 3.4. The Skills Barometer

Latest results from the 2017 Skills Barometer shows that employment is going to increase in the next decade in Northern Ireland. However most of the new job opportunities will be filled by people already in the labour market. The remaining jobs will be filled either by people currently in education or new migrants. This second component is harder to anticipate also in relation to Brexit.

Estimates show that the demand for high skilled people is going to increase while the demand for low skilled people is expected to decrease meaning that achieving higher levels of qualifications increases the chances of being employed.

Analysis of people with high levels of qualifications (NQF Level 6 and above) shows that students are unevenly distributed across fields of study. More precisely, there is an undersupply of graduates in engineering and technology, maths and computer science, physical and environmental sciences (mainly STEM subjects) while there an oversupply of students in fields like education, social studies and law, which are relevant mainly for jobs in the public sector.

However, District Councils have become increasingly involved in skills development planning, particularly through their Community Plans which involves discussion with local employers on their skills needs. For example, Armagh City, Banbridge and Craigavon Council recent Employability and Skills Strategy for the Borough involved extensive consultation with employers on their skills needs. To understand this better, DfE has commissioned UUEPC to develop a sub-regional Skills Barometer that will forecast the future demand for skills on a geographic bases across NI.

As mentioned previously, Sector Skills Councils continue to provide sector specific advice on skills development for employees doing particular jobs. They are independent employer led organisations that provide a range of services to help employers to reduce skills shortages and improve learning standards. Any of the Sector Bodies/Sector Councils involve representation from business and therefore engagement with business in terms of their skills needs.

Promoting inclusive growth in the labour market

Focus on the low skilled or disadvantaged

Providing people with the skills needed in the labour market as well as bringing economically inactive people in the workforce are seen as a priority in the *Draft Programme for Government Framework (*PfG). Nearly a third of the 134 training programmes reviewed by the Department for the Economy as part of its employer engagement review are dedicated to employability skills and NQF level 1 qualifications. This has been identified as a potential area of duplication for the Department which noted that 'a significant variation in outcomes and impacts' had been reported across the programmes. Further work is being undertaken on this issue.

In support of the Draft PfG, the Economy 2030 strategy notes that improving the skills and employability of those who face the greatest barriers to accessing the labour markets will remain a priority (Department for the Economy, 2016[13]). It also recognises the importance of reducing NI's historically high levels of economic inactivity, setting a target of helping 18 000 economically inactive people back to work by 2021. In order to achieve this, the strategy makes the following commitments:

- Supporting those who need help to access the skills that will help them compete for employment opportunities;

- Helping those furthest away from work so that they can take full advantage of employment opportunities and contribute to NI's future prosperity;

- Proactively supporting those furthest from the workforce, removing barriers, providing access to skills and encouraging participation;

- Increasing the number of economically inactive claimants taking up formal programmes of support to develop and improve their skills levels and help them into work;

A number of other public sector strategies also have targets related to the commitments above. These include:

- The Skills Strategy for NI (2011) - Success through Skills – Transforming Futures, aims to 'increase levels of social inclusion by enhancing the employability of those currently excluded from the labour market' (Department for Employment and Learning, 2011[30]).

- The Further Education Strategy (2016) states it will **'s**upport social inclusion by providing those with low or no qualifications, or who have barriers to learning, with the skills and qualifications needed to find employment and to become economically active' (Department for Employment and Learning, 2016[31]).

Northern Ireland has made considerable progress in implementing social clauses, due to the work that the Central Procurement Directorate (CPD) conducted particularly in the construction sector to get agreement on a model for including apprenticeships in all construction contracts. In November 2015 the Procurement Board agreed the Strategic Review of Social Clauses and the Buy Social Construction model for implementation from April 2016. From April 2016 the Buy Social requirements are to be used in procurement above £2m for construction and above £4m for civil engineering contracts.

For example, the Steps to Success contracts provide employment support for the long-term unemployed to help them enter the labour market and sustain employment. The contracts are for 4 years with a possible extension, and commenced in October 2014. They are based on a high degree of payment by results: contractors are paid an attachment fee when a person is referred to them, a job-placement fee when that person enters employment, and then additional outcome payments when the person is still in employment after 6, 9 and 12 months. There are no guaranteed numbers of referrals but the tender process is based on assumed volumes and assumed proportions of starters that progress to sustained employment.

In terms of social benefit requirements, the specification for the contracts set out the following employment and training requirements:

- Objective 1: The Contractor will provide a minimum of 936 Person Weeks of paid employment opportunities for a long-term unemployed person(s), either directly or through its supply chain, within the four (4) year period of the contract, to be arranged throughout the contract lot in Northern Ireland.

- Objective 2: The Contractor will provide a minimum of 936 Person Weeks for apprentices on formally recognised paid apprenticeships within the four (4) year period of the contract, either directly through its workforce or through the workforce of the supply chain (with 20 or more employees). An apprenticeship is one that is delivered within the framework of the DEL ApprenticeshipsNI programme, or equivalent subsequent programme.

- Objective 3: The Contractor and their supply chain shall provide opportunities for all employees to develop essential skills, for example, through the promotion of DEL Essential Skills–Programme.

The Draft Programme for Government emphasises the importance of targeting the economically inactive and more vulnerable people in Northern Ireland. In particular, the initiatives should support transition into work and will involve a wide range of stakeholders including a number of government departments, the local government, the voluntary and community sectors and the employers. This initiative includes a suite of programmes and services to support people to find work and employers to fill jobs which will be in place from 2018 and to develop a new pattern of school-to-employer engagement for pupils to gain an understanding of what the world of work looks like.

Focus on key sectors

The government also commits to a *"Local Works"* approach to improving employability through the "Buy Social" partnership with the local government. This initiative takes a sectoral approach to employability creating a pipeline to better match skills supply and demand in key sectors. It recognises that a *'one size fits all'* approach does not work at the regional level and therefore focuses on tailored solutions to the specific skills needs of each council area. It is aimed at economically inactive people, working with all councils, with a specific focus in areas of disadvantage. It involves working with the sectoral skills bodies, local councils and the DfE to design and implement an "employability pipeline" model similar to those trialled in Scotland where jobs in specific sectors (an initial focus on hospitality/tourism, caring and retail) are ring-fenced for economically inactive clients who are then supported to access these through skills development, employability and mentoring provision.

Where a Forum does not exist government commits to establish, with support from DE, DfE and local partners, an Employability Forum in each council area to effectively bring about a change in how better match the supply and demand for work, through the Community Planning process.

Gas to the West is a result of a social clause requiring contractors to provide apprenticeships, training, and work experience opportunities for "new entrant trainees" in the construction and gas engineering sectors. A number of Councils have made a commitment to promote employment and skills development among low-skilled and disadvantaged people in their areas. For example, Belfast City Council have committed to deliver a *'Belfast Employability Pathway Model'* as part of their Belfast Agenda which is a scalable integrated whole life programme that will support those furthest from the labour market through to employment. The Council is working with employers to identify, plan and prepare for emerging job opportunities and to create effective pathways to employment. One example is the Hospitality Employment Academy, an employability programme to help unemployed residents across the city to develop the necessary skills needed to gain employment opportunities within the hospitality sector. The academy includes a two-week intensive training programme to give participants the skills they need to access a range of entry-level positions within the hospitality sector. In addition to developing new skills participants are matched to employment opportunities and as a minimum are guaranteed interviews with employers with job opportunities available.

Employer engagement in delivering VET at the local level

The role of employers in influencing training provision

Northern Ireland has been relatively slow to develop a culture of employer engagement in skills development with much of past focus being on the supply of skills rather than on demand. This has led to a misalignment of skills and has also meant that the education and training system has been slow to respond to the rapidly changing labour markets as a consequence of digitalisation. There are now around 8 to 9 mainstream employer engagement programmes and upwards on 160 employer engagement programmes operating at both a regional and Council levels. Queen's University and Ulster University have dedicated employer engagement units as does many of the Further Education Colleges in terms of business development support.

The local Further Education colleges are playing an increasingly important role in working with employers to develop programmes/courses locally. One local employer interface initiative is the 'GET Engineering Cluster' which is a college-industry partnership that includes 76 indigenous and international companies and South West College (SWC). The cluster meets monthly and has directly influenced the development of a suite of GOLD Level 3 and Higher Level Apprenticeships along with an annual 'GET Engineering' careers fair. This college-industry partnership has led to a fully aligned system where the curriculum, provision and services provided by a regional College is aligned with the demands of the manufacturing sector.

Another programme is called the Bridge to Employment and provides customised training to unemployed people to give them the skills necessary to compete for new employment opportunities. The programmes are run in response to employers with job vacancies so the training is tailored to meet the skills needed for that job. These are directly focused on what the company needs.

The sectoral partnerships are also a way of giving employers influence over programmes with aim of giving young people the right qualifications/skills. The curriculum is key here. An example given is the Hospitality and Catering sector which worked with the Department to ensure that the curriculum and qualifications achieved met the sector's needs. This is challenging because of the number of steps to go through. Any modification to course content/ qualification has to go through a regulator and this takes time and effort. In terms of full-time education, there are advisory boards in the schools made up of a wide range of stakeholders including employers.

There are mechanisms in place through some of the projects/programmes and working groups involved in skills development in Northern Ireland. For example, with the Public Private Partnerships, a number of Northern Ireland's large and flagship companies including Fujitsu, Capita, Dale Farm and Randox Laboratories are involved. With the Assured Skills Academy model the company selects the trainees to commence the Academy, a pre-employment training programme is designed by the company in conjunction with a local college or university, the training programme is delivered by the college/university with input from the company and the company interviews the trainees at the end of the programme. Examples of Academies include Advanced Cyber Security Analyst, Java, Salesforce, Cloud – using AWS qualification, Data Analytics – both generic and for individual companies, Financial Technology and Software Testers.

The Assured Skills programme seeks to assure potential investors, and existing employers considering expansion, that the skills they need to support a growing business can be found in Northern Ireland. It does this by employing all of DfE's responsibilities for the higher and further education sectors and the Department's skills and training programmes. Assured Skills supports the company's business plan by:

- adding value to their training and skills development activity by facilitating links with the further education and university sectors
- designing pre-employment training solutions
- supporting recruitment and other pre-employment activities

The programme focuses on pre-employment training to graduates. The Academy model is a short-term intervention to help companies meet specific needs. To date, the Programme has up-skilled unemployed graduates in software testing, cloud computing, data analytics, sales & marketing, financial and legal services and professional software skills.

Facilitating the involvement of SMEs

SMEs are a challenge in getting involved. Typically they do not have an explicit HR function so the owner/ management team representative is trying to support skills development doing this. They have limited time and cost is prohibitive. It is mainly a capacity issue. This comes back to the need to provide better education to business on how to use staff more effectively and make more informed decisions around skills development in the company. There is a need to bring employers and educators together. Employers, particularly smaller employers, expect to be beneficiaries but not influencers. They do not understand the language of educators and this needs to be addressed. Ideally it is important to demystify the education language e.g. speaking in 'levels'. A point was made that even the simple terms like 'apprenticeships' evokes different interpretations. Many businesses do not appreciate that this is work-based training.

Understanding the role of local councils in Northern Ireland

Employer engagement in Northern Ireland varies significantly across firm size and sectors. Typically, SMEs have not developed the same capacity to identify and articulate current and future skills needs. The issue concerns especially Northern Ireland's micro businesses, with less than 10 employees that are often challenged by time and resources constraints.

In recent years, under the local government reform, the 11 District Councils in Northern Ireland have taken on a wider role in economic development and skills development. For example, a number of Councils have developed Employability and Skills Strategies which promote partnerships within their Council areas and include a strong focus on the role and involvement of business and employers in supporting economic development priorities locally.

Box 3.5. Implementing a local employment and skills strategy in Northern Ireland

Armagh City, Banbridge and Craigavon (ABC) Borough Council have developed an Employability and Skills Strategy, which has a strong employer engagement focus to include a role in an Employability and Skills Forum within the Borough to provide input into the skills needs of the area. This also includes membership from government, the private sector, training and education providers and others. ABC's Skills Strategy also has a sectoral focus, recommending the introduction of a competitive bursary scheme for local SMEs in the Council area's 5 priority sectors - Digital and Creative Technologies, Advanced Manufacturing, Materials and Engineering; Life and Health Sciences; Agri-Food; and Tourism – which focuses on re-skilling and up-skilling the existing workforce within the ABC Borough Council area.

Some local Councils have also made a strong commitment to employer engagement through their Community Plans. Each Council has developed a Community Plan which sets out the long-term vision for the social, economic and environmental development of their area. This includes the unique selling points for the area to help attract business investment and growth. A wide range of partners, including representatives from the business, statutory, higher education, community and voluntary sectors, have worked with each Council to develop their Community Plans.

For example, Belfast City Council's Community Plan is called the *'Belfast Agenda'* and it makes a number of commitments around employment and skills which actively engages the business community (Belfast City, 2016[32]). This includes a draft Employability and Skills framework 2015-2025 whose vision is to *'realise the potential of Belfast's economy and its people by transforming skills, employability and aspiration, resulting in higher levels of business growth, employment and incomes'*. This includes engagement with employers on a number of levels including Academies working with local construction companies involved in Belfast City Council capital projects and paid work experience for students in sectors including IT and creative and digital technologies.

Derry City Council makes a commitment in its Community Plan to develop a community that is *'better skilled and educated'* and this includes an action to increase industry engagement in careers advice and guidance.

Mid Ulster Council has established a Mid Ulster Skills Forum charged with understanding and communicating the needs of employers and investors in the District relating to skills gaps and employability issues which impact on the economic wellbeing of the area, and identifying and implementing appropriate actions through partners to improve provision and support. Representatives from a wide range of local employers, further education colleges and business organisations have been involved in devising the terms of reference and programme of work for the Forum. The Forum is chaired by a Director with one of the region's largest employers, Dunbia, which is a meat processing plant.

Box 3.6. Area Learning Communities

Area learning communities (ALCs) are voluntary coalition of schools in different areas focused on providing a real opportunity to develop the Entitlement Framework and a shared responsibility for its delivery to all the young people in an area by providing them with access to a wide range of learning opportunities suited to their needs, aptitudes and interests, irrespective of where they live or the school they attend. They came in recognition that each school cannot provide every subject/course and ensure that the curriculum could be planned on an area basis. All of the post primary schools in NI are members of ALCs. From September 2017, schools have to offer pupils access to a minimum of 21 courses at Key Stage 4 and 21 courses at post-16. At least one third of these courses should be general and at least one third applied (with more practical content). A growing number of schools are now engaged with their local College in innovative and creative approaches to collaborative working. There are currently 30 ALCs established across the Northern Ireland within which 250 schools and Colleges are working to increase the range of courses for pupils in the local area. This has opened up many more occupational studies at local Further Education colleges for students.

Flexibility of public institutions in responding to local employer needs

Most businesses are very busy so tend to engage with public institutions only when the need them. More sophisticated businesses naturally behave more strategically and are well switched on to engaging with, for example, the universities. This is evident from the lists of businesses that tend to engage in, for example, the Higher Level Apprenticeships. Smaller companies are less likely to approach their local college or equivalent for support.

Business in the Community is a UK business-led membership organisation made up of businesses of all sizes who understand that the prosperity of business and society are mutually dependent. Business in the Community in Northern Ireland has a wide range of employer engagement programmes which brings together employers with the skills and education system in Northern Ireland. This includes supporting about 10,000 placements a year of school children with employers which more recently has focused on 'Work Inspiration' days in companies which allow children to see in practical terms how a business works. This is an inclusive programme open to children across all schools in Northern Ireland. Previously school placements were organised on an ad hoc basis and were difficult for children from more marginal communities to access.

Colleges have been working flexibly with the Department through the Assured Skills Programme. A good example is provided by Belfast Met and e3. The aims of e3 are to enhance the employability and skills of learners, support enterprise through incubation and small business programmes and foster innovative approaches to economic development. The services offered from this facility and across the colleges include customer training programmes and support for enterprise development. They deliver innovation voucher programmes with the support of Invest NI, product development and apprenticeships. They operate across a range of sectors including composites, financial services, tourism, retail, health and life sciences, and digital and ICT.

One of the key component parts and innovations in e3 is FRESH, the project-based learning approach that e3 has piloted. That is a new approach that is embedded in the curriculum and is focused on enhancing students' creativity and innovation skills within their curriculum and across all higher education programmes. In the Titanic Quarter, they are working on larger-scale business engagement, looking at offshore energy and a bioskills academy. They are also delivering the employer support programme, which is funded by DEL, and are working with Invest NI on developing a new cluster called the energy skills training network.

Box 3.7. The Council for Curriculum, Examinations and Assessment

The Council for Curriculum, Examinations and Assessment (CCEA) responded to the needs of the growing Life and Health Sciences sector in Northern Ireland by introducing a unique and innovative A level in Life and Health Sciences, for first teaching from September 2016. The sector, comprising of 130 companies and employing approximately 23,000 people, generates around £800m in sales per annum, accounting for approximately 25% of Northern Ireland's economic output. The qualification was a response to the findings of a key report by the Northern Ireland Science Industry Panel. The Matrix report on Life & Health Sciences in Northern Ireland (2015) identified that the vast and expanding Life & Health Sciences sector requires a highly skilled scientific workforce for projected future job growth. CCEA responded to the needs of the sector and its current recruitment shortfall by working collaboratively with key employers to design a very relevant and engaging qualification. The new qualification has been developed in consultation with the major companies such as Almac, Norbrook and Intelesens and will give students an opportunity to develop critical skills demanded by a growing industry.

An American company, Bemis, recently announced that it was establishing a European Business Service Centre in Campsie, Derry~Londonderry creating up to 95 positions. To help recruit for these roles, in partnership with the Department for the Economy and NWRC, Bemis launched a five-week Global Business Services Academy to equip participants with the skills required to fulfil business financial service roles in the new Centre. The participants who were all previously educated to HND or Degree level gained industry recognised qualifications as a result of the five-week programme.

The Higher Level Apprenticeship (HLA) concept has involved over 600 participants across 40 occupational areas including ICT, engineering, accounting and digital marketing. HLAs currently offer qualifications from Level 4 to Level 6 (Honours degree). The majority are at Level 5 (Foundation degree). They enable employers to train staff to the level required as well as assuring that there are people available with strong technical and good employability skills. Staff are trained to the employer's specific requirements, apprentices can help fill skills gaps increasing productivity and securing a high calibre of staff for the business. The Metropolitan and Regional Colleges, Open University and University of Ulster can respond quick rapidly to employer requests in terms of HLAs.

Benefits of training for employers

There does not appear to be any formal mechanism for employers to report the benefits of training in Northern Ireland. From experience, employers find it difficult to assess and articulate the benefits of training. This does seem to be a particular weakness in trying to help companies to determine and appreciate the impact of training on sales and productivity which is of particular importance for Northern Ireland.

There is extensive use of case studies to highlight the benefit of certain programmes. This includes, for example, Academies and Higher Level Apprenticeships. Evaluations are undertaken of each programme which would include providing quantitative and qualitative outcomes for employers of engaging in those programmes. It is unlikely that those benefits are fed back to employers.

Apprenticeships in non-traditional fields

Apprenticeships are offered in non-traditional fields, particularly in terms of higher-level apprenticeships. For example, Deloitte recently launched a new Robotics Automation Academy, offering over 20 graduates the opportunity to join its Belfast office. The Department for the Economy has backed the scheme which is a 12-week training programme delivered by Belfast Met. Those candidates who are successful will gain an industry recognised qualification and a potential offer of employment from Deloitte.

Currently there are around 170 Level 2 and Level 3 apprenticeships and over 45 Higher Level Apprenticeships to choose from, including computer science, life sciences, accountancy and digital marketing. Apprenticeships include built environment services, creative industry skills including costume and wardrobe and cultural heritage along with hospitality and catering including front-of-house and hospitality supervision.

Tailored / ad-hoc training courses

There is an opportunity to access short-term bespoke training under the Assured Skills "Academy Model". Where a company or a consortium of companies have an identified skills need, DfE will consider developing a short-term pre-employment training intervention to meet that need. This typically involves an eight to ten week pre-employment training programme delivered by a local college or university, followed by a four to six week placement with a participating company. The intervention is designed to lower the recruitment risk for companies by providing candidates trained with the initial skills for the opportunities that are available.

The Academy Model is flexible and versatile, and has been used to help companies recruit new staff in areas such as data analytics, human resources, legal services, financial services, sales, software development, software testing, cyber security, welding, control numerical control machining, 2D animation and game development. The benefits of the Academy Model for companies include:

- assistance with recruitment and selection (including psychometric assessment if required);

- a pre-employment training programme designed by the company or companies in conjunction with a local college or university;
- the training programme delivered by the college/university with input from the companies;
- the company interview the trainees at the end of the programme; and
- the Department meets almost all of the costs associated with the intervention.

The Academy recruits students from a wide range of backgrounds including the unemployed, under-employed, school leavers, graduates or have experience and would like to change career direction. However, the vast majority of Academy programmes have been aimed at providing graduate level opportunities for unemployed graduates. Over the last two years alone, the Academies have helped graduates secure jobs in diverse sectors such as data analytics, human resources, financial services, sales, software development, software testing, cyber security, 2D animation and game development.

The Academies have over 80% success rate of participants progressing into full time employment. Current academies are advertised in local newspapers and online resources including jobcentreonline, nidirect, NIJobs, recruitNI and social media.

For example, the Software Testers' Academy was the first Academy Model programme. Four cohorts have taken place since 2011, and almost 40 different companies, both large and small, have used the Software Testers' Academy to meet their recruitment needs.

Improving work organisation, job design and skills utilisation in the workplace

Most public policies have largely focused on boosting the supply of skills, namely the number of people with vocational or academic qualifications. However, there is an increasing recognition within the OECD that more should be done to work with employers to look at the use of skills in the workplace. Skills utilisation concerns the extent to which skills are effectively applied in the workplace to maximise employer and individual performance. As such it involves a mix of policies including work organisation, job design, technology adaptation, innovation, employee-employer relations, human resource development practices and business product market strategies (OECD/ILO, 2017[21])

It is often at the local level where the interface of these factors can best be addressed. Policies which aim to improve skills use in the workplace can help address the multi-faceted challenges many local economies are facing and contribute to national productivity and inclusive growth objectives. There are a series of internal and external factors that influence the decision of firms about whether to pursue high or low road employment strategies. These strategies can become self-reinforcing not only at the level of individual workplaces, but also within a local labour market.

> **Box 3.8. The UK Business Productivity Review**
>
> Raising productivity is one of the Government's key priorities and is core to the UK's Industrial Strategy. The United Kingdom has strong business environment but productivity remains low in comparison to other international peers.
>
> The Industrial Strategy focused on the five dimensions of productivity: ideas, people, infrastructure, business environment and place. The objective of this initiative is to improve productivity for low productive businesses and for those that underperform relative to national and international benchmarks.
>
> The Business Productivity Review analyses also how new technologies, managing practices and business support services by both the public and private sectors can contribute to increase productivity and working conditions of employees.
>
> *Source*: https://www.gov.uk/government/consultations/business-productivity-review-call-for-evidence.

High-performance workplaces and work organisation in Northern Ireland

Examining workplace practices often associated with higher levels of skills use can also provide useful indications of the degree to which skills are being put to good use. Skills use is generally associated with High-Performance Work Practices (HPWP), which include such things as employee award programmes, flexible job descriptions, regular performance appraisals as well as mentoring and leadership development courses in the workplace. About 20% of jobs in Northern Ireland are characterised by high levels of High-Performance Work Practices, well below that of OECD countries like Sweden, Austria, Finland, Denmark as well as the region of England.

Figure 3.1. High-performance work practices across OECD countries

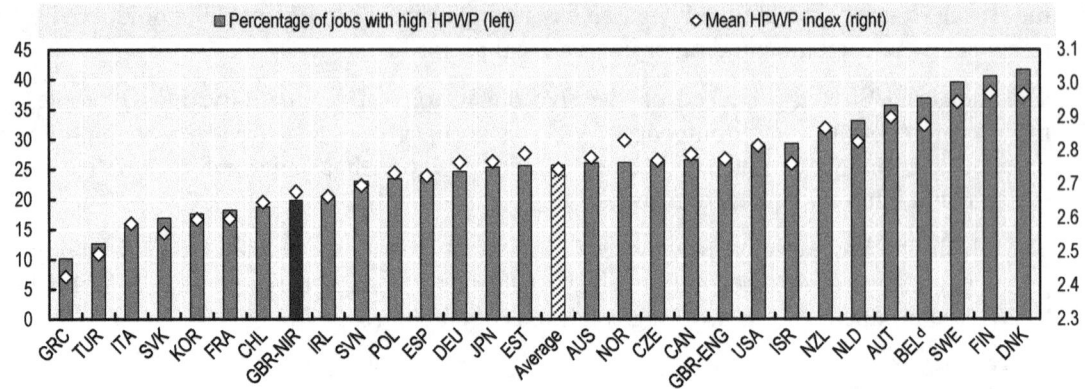

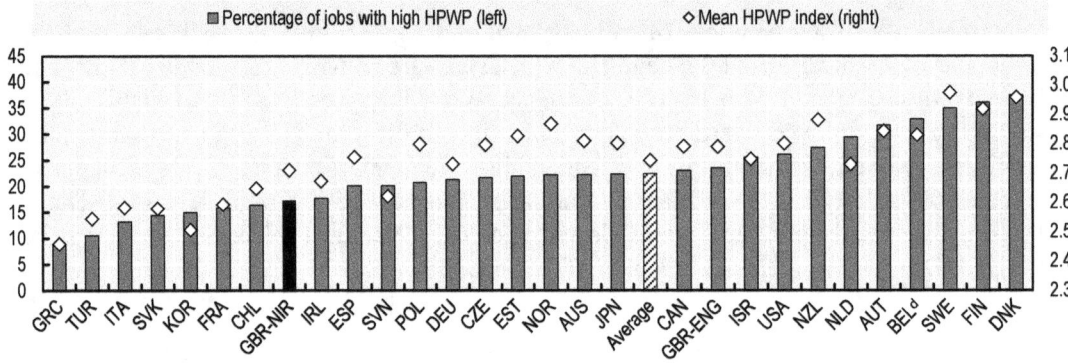

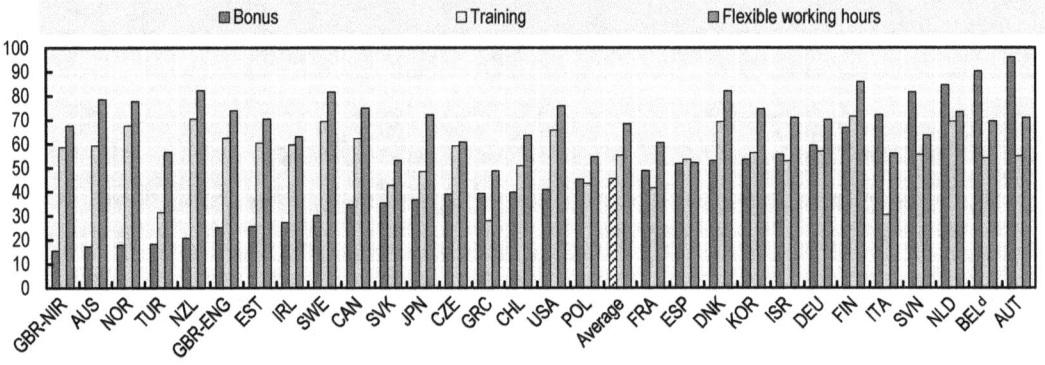

Source: OECD Survey of Adult skills (PIAAC) database, 2012 and 2015

StatLink https://doi.org/10.1787/888933903574

A number of factors can influence the degree to which skills are put to good use within the firm. Product market strategies are fundamental to understanding the quality of jobs and the potential for firms to better use the skills of their employees. The nature of the business and the competitive advantages pursued can also impact the level and types of skills that employers seek and use. Product market strategies (PMS) describe the ways in which private sector establishments choose to differentiate and position the products and services they provide within the markets in which they operate (United Kingdom Commission for Employment and Skills, 2016[33]). As companies move into higher value-added product and service markets, the levels of skills that they require, and the extent to which they utilise skills, tends to increase. Evidence from the 2016 UK Commission for Employment and Skills Employer Survey shows 23% of responding employer report very low product market strategies (see Figure 3.2) (United Kingdom Commission for Employment and Skills, 2016[33]). This is an index developed within the survey, which assigns a score of 1-5 based on the following factors:

- the extent to which their competitive success depended on price;
- the extent to which the establishment tended to lead the way in their industry in terms of the development of new products, materials or techniques;
- the extent to which the establishment competed in a 'premium quality' product market as opposed to a 'standard or basic quality' product market; and
- the extent to which they offered goods or services with a substantial amount of customisation according to customer requirements.

Figure 3.2. Product market strategies, UK countries, 2015

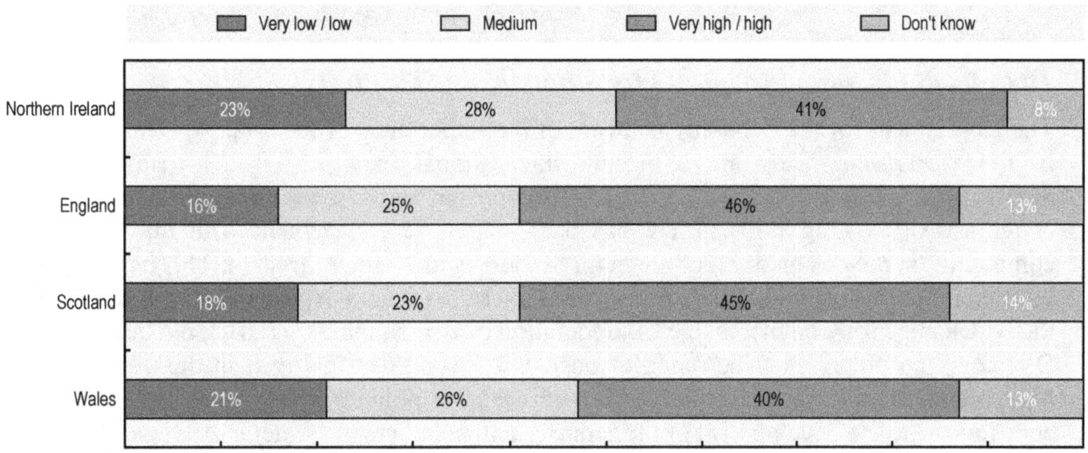

	Very low / low	Medium	Very high / high	Don't know
Northern Ireland	23%	28%	41%	8%
England	16%	25%	46%	13%
Scotland	18%	23%	45%	14%
Wales	21%	26%	40%	13%

Source: UKCES Employer Skills Survey 2015.

StatLink https://doi.org/10.1787/888933903593

Figure 3.3 shows the share of enterprise that have introduced new methods of work organisation from 2012-14 within regions of the United Kingdom based on data from the UK Innovation Survey. While the survey results showed a general decrease among firms in undertaking innovative activities between 2012 and 2014, Northern Ireland employers trail most regions in the UK with only 18% of firms reporting new methods of work organisation (Department for Business, Energy & Industrial Strategy, 2018[34]).

Figure 3.3. Share of enterprises that introduced new methods of organising work responsibilities, NUTS2 regions of the UK, 2012-2014

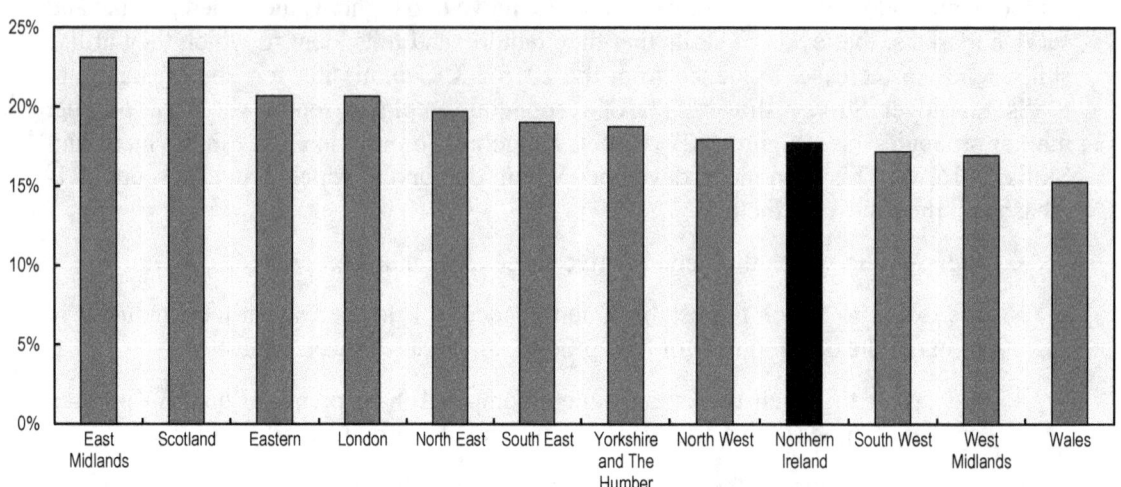

Note: The chart shows establishments that used for the first time a new system of employee responsibilities, team work, decentralisation, integration or de-integration of departments, education / training systems etc.
Source: Department for Business, Energy & Industrial Strategy (2016), UK Innovation Survey

StatLink https://doi.org/10.1787/888933903612

The role of the public sector in promoting better skills use

The Department for the Economy is aware of the importance of fostering better skills use in the workplace. They are exploring international examples from Australia and Scandinavian countries on how to improve job design and support companies to make a better use of existing skills. There has been extensive engagement with the business community in the design of all of the main Strategies in Northern Ireland. This has largely been facilitated through the various business bodies operating in Northern Ireland including the NI Chamber of Commerce, the Confederation of British Industry (CBI), the Institute of Directors and others. A wide range of businesses were also involved in the design and implementation of apprenticeships and youth training policies. They made a significant contribution to the development of the Strategy and members of Strategic Advisory Forum were selected from these groups.

Invest NI are involved in a number of programmes and interventions to improve work organisation and the use of existing skills. The Invest NI Skills Intervention Programme has provided a range of interventions to supported businesses in order to assist them to become *'more competitive by developing the skills of their staff to create a skilled, trained and adaptable workforce, thereby improving the capabilities of the businesses, people and processes."* Over the last seven years the Programme has included the following core elements:

1. Business Improvement Training Programme (BITP) programme

2. Skills Growth Programme comprising the Skills Growth Programme Grant (SGP) for larger projects, and Skills Advancement Grant (SAG) for small projects and

3. Training Needs Analysis (TNA) Workshops/Mentoring

The SGP replaced BITP in 2013 and was largely based upon BITP in terms of the specific nature of the support given, with the main variation being that a specific small project support – SAG - was also introduced in 2013. This was to address concerns that small companies were not availing sufficiently of the programme. The Skills Intervention Programme has been open to a wide range of Invest NI client businesses in both manufacturing and internationally tradable services. It has formed part of a wider support package to attract new FDI. Awards cover both standalone projects and those as part of wider expansion and investment plans. Three collaborative projects have also been also supported.

Financial support through the Programme has focused on providing specific training directly related to employee tasks within the business and to general training to enhance the skills of the workforce more widely. The Programme has required companies to align their proposed training activity across four broad themes namely management development, technical skills, soft skills and functional skills. Both external and internal trainers have provided training through the Programme.

Box 3.9. The Curriculum Hub initiative

The Curriculum Hub initiative is a new concept and represents a significant development in the way Further Education colleges deliver education in the priority occupational areas identified in the Industrial Strategy. The initiative sees the designation of a single Further Education college as the Curriculum Hub for a designated curriculum area.

The lead college, acting as the Curriculum Hub, operates in conjunction with the other five local colleges to review the curriculum offer across further education in order to develop coherent pathways, future-scope curriculum, develop Continuing Professional Development at a sector level (including industrial experience), ensure curriculum is developed by appropriately skilled staff and ensure coherent communication and promotion.

This initiative complements developments within Apprenticeship and Youth Training and promotes a more coherent interaction across the Department to enhance engagement with employers and further education.

The following Curriculum Hubs have been allocated to Further Education colleges:

- Belfast Met – Digital and ICT;
- South West College – Advanced Manufacturing;
- Southern Regional College – Life Sciences
- South Eastern Regional College – Construction and
- North West Regional College – Health and Social Care

Applications to be designated as the lead hub in hospitality & tourism are currently being assessed with an announcement pending in December 2018.

Focus on better using skills within SMEs

The Employer Support Programme, encompassing Skills Focus and InnovateUs, has been designed to support the needs of the small to medium sized business in mind and as such offers a flexible training solution in terms of times, class size and also the location of delivery, which can take place within the workplace or at the local college. A skills audit is conducted for all employer engagement under the Employer Support context.

Skills Focus has been developed to increase the skills levels and employability of employees within the existing workforce. It aims to support, promote and facilitate collaborative work between business and FE colleges in order to provide tailored skills provision to small to medium sized enterprises with less than 250 employees.

The purpose of Skills Focus is to meet business needs by increasing the skills levels of the existing workforce to level 2 and above qualifications. The programme allows a tailored training solution for SMEs to upskill the existing workforce. Each project will require a 25% employer contribution and requires the college to invoice the employer for 25% of the cost.

InnovateUs aims to encourage and promote opportunities for businesses and FE colleges to work together (Belfast Met, 2018[35]). In particular, the focus of the programme is to enable small businesses, with fewer than 50 employees, to acquire the skills necessary to engage in innovation activities. The programme has been designed with the needs of small businesses in mind and to be flexible in meeting these needs, for example to fit with businesses working patterns. As part of this flexibility, the training to be delivered can take place within the workplace or at the college. The role of those programmes is to support the company around how to go about addressing skills needs. Sectors it is involved with include Advanced Engineering & Manufacturing, Health & Life Sciences, Food, Drink & Tourism, ICT and Renewable Energy & Sustainable Technologies. For example, through the South Eastern Regional College O.D Cars, which specialises in a range of engine re-manufacturing, benefited from bespoke, one-to-one CNC techniques and computer aided design mentoring. The business also gained access to resources which have helped them undertake innovation activities, improve their business with new technologies and remain competitive. It would seem from the research however that less emphasis appears go into educating employers on what their skills needs, particularly future needs, are/should be.

In addition to an extensive range of Further and Higher Education Courses, the Economic Engagement Teams across Northern Ireland's Regional Colleges aim to encourage local economic development by supporting companies, large or small, in the social economy, private or public sector, to help them find solutions to their training and development needs. Their focus is to support business through the provision of four integrated services – upskilling, innovation, apprenticeship and start-up.

Local strategies to encourage better skills use in the workplace

Investors in People (IIP) operate in Northern Ireland and help evaluate business internal performance over time and identify areas for further investment. The evaluation is based on an online assessment including 27 scales for comparison. IIP also offers the ability to benchmark against the industry average. The Investors in People framework is designed around the key three principles that make up the Standard; Leading, Supporting and Improving. These key strands are then broken down further to pinpoint the things that any given organisation does well in terms of its people management, whilst understanding where they're going wrong, and helping to innovate ways to improve. In essence, IIP is built to add value to a business by helping build strategies to encourage the best from its employees. IIP do use case studies of local companies to demonstrate the benefits of taking the IIP approach. This includes a company called Colorite which highlighted how the new standard applies people engagement practices in order for the organisation to achieve their long term objectives.

IIP used to be part of Northern Ireland government through the Department of Employment and Learning (DEL) but is now a community interest company which is 49% owned by the Department of Education (UK). There are 557 organisations with IIP in Northern Ireland. Various Councils, Business Bodies and Media host business award ceremonies, some of which include a focus on skills e.g. Belfast Telegraph Excellence in the Development of Management & Leadership award.

References

Belfast City (2016), *Your Future City: The Belfast Agenda*. [12]

Belfast Met (2018), *Innovate Us*, http://www.belfastmet.ac.uk/support-for-business/employer-support/innovate-us/. [16]

Department for Business, Energy & Industrial Strategy (2018), *UK Innovation Survey 2017*, Department for Business, Energy & Industrial Strategy. [15]

Department for Employment and Learning (2016), *Further education Means Success: The Northern Ireland Strategy for Further Education*, https://www.economy-ni.gov.uk/sites/default/files/publications/economy/FE-Strategy%20-FE-Means-success.pdf (accessed on 23 October 2018). [11]

Department for Employment and Learning (2011), *Success through Skills-Transforming Futures*, https://www.economy-ni.gov.uk/sites/default/files/publications/economy/Success-through-Skills-Transforming-Futures.pdf (accessed on 25 October 2018). [10]

Department for the Economy (2016), *Economy 2030: A consultation on an Industrial Strategy for Northern Ireland*, https://www.economy-ni.gov.uk/sites/default/files/consultations/economy/industrial-strategy-ni-consultation-document.pdf (accessed on 25 October 2018). [9]

Department for the Economy((n.d.)), *Careers Advisory Forum*, https://www.economy-ni.gov.uk/publications/careers-advisory-forum (accessed on 25 October 2018). [5]

Department for the Economy((n.d.)), *Northern Ireland Skills Barometer 2017 Update*, https://www.economy-ni.gov.uk/publications/ni-skills-barometer (accessed on 25 October 2018). [8]

Department for the Economy((n.d.)), *Preparing for success*, https://www.economy-ni.gov.uk/publications/preparing-success (accessed on 25 October 2018). [4]

Department of education((n.d.)), *STEM strategy | Department of Education*, https://www.education-ni.gov.uk/articles/stem-strategy (accessed on 25 October 2018). [1]

Education and Training Inspectorate (2016), *Chief Inspector's Report 2014-2016*, https://www.etini.gov.uk/sites/etini.gov.uk/files/publications/CIR%20Report%20November%202016.pdf (accessed on 25 October 2018). [7]

Invest NI (2015), *Collaborative Networks Programme Collaborative Network Programme Application Guidance Notes*, https://secure.investni.com/static/library/invest-ni/phase-3/collaborative-networks-call/collaborative-application-guidance-notes.pdf (accessed on 25 October 2018). [2]

OECD (2014), *Employment and Skills Strategies in Northern Ireland, United Kingdom*, OECD Reviews on Local Job Creation, OECD Publishing, Paris, http://dx.doi.org/10.1787/9789264208872-en. [3]

OECD/ILO (2017), *Better Use of Skills in the Workplace: Why It Matters for Productivity and Local Jobs*, OECD Publishing, Paris, http://dx.doi.org/10.1787/9789264281394-en. [13]

The Education and Training Inspectorate (2016), *Chief Inspectorate's Report 2014-16*, The Education and Training Inspectorate. [6]

United Kingdom Commission for Employment and Skills (2016), *Employer Skills Survey 2015*, UKCES. [14]

ORGANISATION FOR ECONOMIC CO-OPERATION AND DEVELOPMENT

The OECD is a unique forum where governments work together to address the economic, social and environmental challenges of globalisation. The OECD is also at the forefront of efforts to understand and to help governments respond to new developments and concerns, such as corporate governance, the information economy and the challenges of an ageing population. The Organisation provides a setting where governments can compare policy experiences, seek answers to common problems, identify good practice and work to co-ordinate domestic and international policies.

The OECD member countries are: Australia, Austria, Belgium, Canada, Chile, the Czech Republic, Denmark, Estonia, Finland, France, Germany, Greece, Hungary, Iceland, Ireland, Israel, Italy, Japan, Korea, Latvia, Lithuania, Luxembourg, Mexico, the Netherlands, New Zealand, Norway, Poland, Portugal, the Slovak Republic, Slovenia, Spain, Sweden, Switzerland, Turkey, the United Kingdom and the United States. The European Union takes part in the work of the OECD.

OECD Publishing disseminates widely the results of the Organisation's statistics gathering and research on economic, social and environmental issues, as well as the conventions, guidelines and standards agreed by its members.

www.ingramcontent.com/pod-product-compliance
Lightning Source LLC
LaVergne TN
LVHW061945070526
838199LV00060B/3977